D0119485

ENJOYING SCOTLAND

ENJOYING SCOTLAND

CAMPBELL STEVEN

ROBERT HALE · LONDON

Robert Hale & Company
63 Old Brompton Road
London S.W.7

Printed in Great Britain by
Lowe & Brydone (Printers) Ltd, Thetford, Norfolk

CONTENTS

ILLUSTRATIONS

ILLUSTRATIONS

All photographs taken by the author

MAPS

For
Helen, John and Kenneth

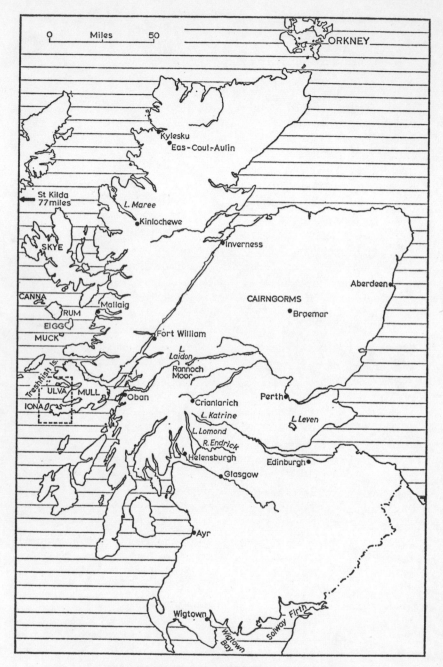

For the **ULVA-IONA** area see page 23.

INTRODUCTION

In attempting to write a book made up of reminiscences of days spent in one's own country, it is inevitably a problem to know just where to begin and where to end. Finally in this instance, rather than go back to the mists of long before yesterday, it was decided to make a purely arbitrary choice and settle for an overall span of the last dozen years. The one exception to this was the day on the Crianlarich hills—described in 'The Ridges' —which dates from a slightly earlier period, when the miles were a little shorter and the gradients rather less steep.

For the most part the enjoyment has come from outings and expeditions sufficiently out of the usual to make the planning of them almost as memorable as their execution; unorthodoxy nearly always brings rewards out of all proportion to the effort involved, and in Scotland, when it is applied to the 'off' season, there are the added advantages that the quiet places are easier to discover and, more often than not, the weather is better.

Yet the days here described have in them nothing too far removed from what anyone may attempt. Indeed it is hoped that they will be taken as examples worth following and that others will find in similar planning and performance as much sheer enjoyment as we have.

My grateful thanks are due to many: to Beaufort (Air-Sea) Equipment Ltd., Birkenhead, for the generous loan of one of their 3Y inflatable dinghies; to the Chief Transport and Movements Officer, Headquarters Scotland (Army), for authorising and making possible a landing-craft trip to St. Kilda; to Mr. Comyn Webster, Editor of *Scottish Field*, for his permission to draw on material already used in article form; and finally to all my various long-suffering companions, certainly not forgetting Mr. Robert McGuffie, Wigtown wildfowler; Mr. Gordon Grant, farmer on Iona; and Mr. Alick Macfarlane, Loch Lomond island postman.

I

The Saltings

That night as I lay awake, I suddenly heard the magic sound of geese and ran to the window, and from over towards the marsh came the call of the Pinkfeet. There must have been a big lot on the move, for the sound seemed like a single singing roar made dim by the two miles of marsh that lay between.

Next morning we stood on the shore. There was an orange glow in the east, and out of it came skein after skein of geese. Since then I have seen Pink-footed Geese in flight many thousands of times in all their winter haunts in Britain; I have followed them to their breeding grounds in Iceland, I have assisted at the capture and ringing of more than 20,000 of them; and yet the thrill which I felt on that first morning is repeated again every time I see the great skeins stretched across the sky. The spell is as strong as ever.

Peter Scott

IT was late one autumn evening when we heard the wild geese overhead.

They passed directly above our garden, and their talk as they flew was strong and clear. In the darkness, unfortunately, there was no counting their numbers: there may have been many dozens, possibly even hundreds, in their close-marshalled chevrons. Only here and there could they be made out, black and indistinct against the frosty sparkle of the stars.

For a while after their calling faded we waited outside, hoping that more birds would follow. But none came. Then at length we turned indoors, wondering as we did so where in the far north their long journey had begun. In Iceland probably, or in Greenland; maybe even among the barren wastes of Spitzbergen. Already winter would be setting in there—the frosts, the snow-blizzards, the long dark nights. One could picture readily how, in those last few days before take-off, the geese had grown more and more restive; how finally they had given in to that instinctive wisdom that urges them each autumn to the friendly havens to the south. Now they would be nearing the end of their long flight, planing in to land at the roosts they had known in the past, remembering too, no doubt, the familiar mudflats and the saltings with the rich, succulent grazing.

The mudflats and the saltings. Pinkfeet and greylags flighting with the dawn. The frost-flashing colours of breaking day, beyond the edge of the tide. . . . Almost painfully I was struck by the realisation that all this was something of which I knew virtually nothing, something which I had certainly never seen. Yet here must be one of the most thrilling sights of all our wild bird life, on view morning after morning the winter through. Here surely, not unduly difficult of access, was a whole new world merely waiting to be discovered and enjoyed.

The geese, in passing, had issued their invitation.

The new year came in with one of those superlative days which sometimes occur in the depth of a Scottish winter.

The sun shone free from a sky that was quite literally cloudless, its warmth bringing a hint of the royal promise of spring. In the garden across the street the bare branches of the big ash tree scarcely moved to the touch of the wind. Yet there was no more than the gentlest suggestion of frost. It was the kind of day that made one reflect more than a little enviously that up on the plateau of Ben Nevis visibility must be stretching almost unbelievably far, from the horizon rim of the Outer Isles to the Ochil Hills behind Perth, from Ben Wyvis in the north possibly even to the pencil outline of Ireland.

That was the occasion of our first attempt to learn something about the geese. We set out in the afternoon, replete and lethargic after New Year's Day lunch, taking the road to Aberfoyle. On the far side of the River Forth, just beyond the village of Gartmore, we turned off along the rutted cart-track which cuts across the north-west corner of Gartrenich Moss. Somewhere out towards the Lake of Menteith we knew to look for the grey geese.

It has to be admitted, however, that we made a remarkably poor job of our stalk. It could have been, of course, that the birds were particularly 'edgy' that afternoon, grazing uneasily on the vast flat expanse of the carse; but it was much more probable that shortage of time played havoc with the stealth of our approach. Whatever the reason, the sentries spotted us at extreme range and there in an instant was the whole army of the geese, a swirling black cloud, angrily airborne some hundreds of yards distant. Their protests carried far in the keen January air, although they certainly did not let resentment interfere with the efficiency of their drill. Within seconds they had swung into line, the kinked black thread of their gaggle stretching high against the sky. For a little we were able to watch them wheeling in a safe, wide circle, while the sunlight rippled along their swiftly beating wing-tips. Then, choosing their new direction, they headed east, grew fainter, and finally disappeared far out over Flanders Moss.

The following morning we tried a different quarter. Instead of the familiar country north of the River Clyde, we chose a line to the south, driving through Hamilton to the upland border between Lanarkshire and Ayrshire. Once again the sun was shining, with harder frost than on the previous day, and we could not help wondering why we had never before bothered to explore the watershed hills of the upper reaches of rivers like the Avon and Ayr, Nethan and Douglas. Here was fine country of moors and deep wooded valleys, but it was not goose territory and we certainly had no luck: not a pinkfoot, not a greylag showed itself anywhere near the road. Indeed the only interest, ornithologically speaking, was on the little Glenbuck Loch, the half-mile sheet of water beside the Douglas-Muirkirk road that is so neatly bisected by the Lanarkshire-Ayrshire boundary. Here we saw, and heard, some 200 whooper swans, feeding for the most part well out towards the middle of the loch and escorted by innumerable flotillas of wigeon. For a while we listened to the swans' trumpeting, echoing on the crisp air as merrily as a hunting-horn chorus. Then we moved on to searchings farther afield which even took us quite absurdly to the scree-strewn summit of Tinto and views in the failing light far out over the upper reaches of the Clyde.

But all day long we had glimpsed not a single goose.

After this second, thoroughly well deserved failure, it was abundantly plain that we could have no real hope of seeing the wintering geese unless we went to some genuine trouble to find them. If the birds would not condescend to be where we considered they ought to be, then the skirmishing must be carried right to the heart of their own territory. Due and solemn consideration gave the answer: the obvious thing to do was to visit the most famous of all wildfowl regions in Britain— the Solway.

"Foremost among the Solway coastal resorts," stated the Nature Conservancy monograph *Wildfowl in Great Britain,* "is the 10 square miles of foreshore and merse which lies along the western side of Wigtown Bay. On the upper reaches, in particular, there are extensive areas of salt-marsh, with the Moss of Cree extending inland for a further 2 square miles, and a belt of low-lying farmland beyond. . . . Taken as a whole the area forms a compact unit, with the roost and the feeding grounds convenient to one another, yet large enough to allow for movement in the event of disturbance." Here, surely, on the vast expanse of the saltings, would be greylag and pinkfeet in abundance; perhaps even, to add to the interest, a scattering of Greenland white-fronts.

The fact that my brother Colin happened to live and work in Wigtown seemed a particularly happy coincidence; a more suitable base-camp would have been very difficult to imagine.

"I've never seen so many geese in the Bay as there have been this winter and I've been shooting here all my life."

Robert McGuffie, veteran Wigtown wildfowler, sat back more comfortably in the depths of his armchair and a satisfied smile creased his face. Then, as if to add a dramatic finishing touch, he went on: "There were 3,000 pinkfeet and 500 grey-lag here this afternoon; you're going to be lucky all right."

My brother looked at me as if to say: "Well, there you are; we can't do much better than that. It's what you asked for, isn't it?" I gladly nodded agreement.

Earlier that evening I had driven down to Wigtown, escaping from Glasgow's rush-hour in steady, persistent rain. Once in the heart of Ayrshire, I had felt the wind-buffets on the car growing in strength and glimpsed the sickle moon through ragged, straggling cloud-tatters. Ailsa Craig lighthouse, flashing through the blackness over the Firth, had offered the greeting of an old friend, speeding me on to the lonelier stretch of road over the high moors to Newton Stewart. Now, my

The Loch Arkaig *approaching Mallaig pier*

brother's welcome over, he and I were seated comfortably by the wildfowler's sitting-room fire, awaiting final instructions for the morrow.

But Robert was in no particular hurry to get down to practical details. With the skill of an expert storyteller he believed in a good build-up of background atmosphere.

"Yes," he went on, with obvious enthusiasm, "they're all pinks and greylags here just now. We did have thirteen Canada geese in September and October, but they all went when the shooting started. The white-fronts, too, they're mostly up by Loch Ken, though I did shoot two in the Bay this past winter."

From the immediate past his thoughts went back to more distant days, to memorable exploits in his own strange world at the tide's fringe, to some of the rare bird visitors he had seen from time to time in the Bay, to hard, bitter seasons when snow and frost had made the geese so desperate with hunger that it would have been unthinkable to take advantage of their tameness. We should have liked to prolong our listening pleasantly far into the night, but the arrangement proposed for the following morning was that Robert and I should be out in position on the saltings in good time to see the dawn flight. This, of course, would be an everyday event for him; for me it would be rather less commonplace. While it was still early, therefore, we said good-night.

The darkness was as black as a navvy's tea when I stepped outside shortly before six the next morning. The sky was thickly overcast and the wind, moist and chill, came gusting across the bay from the unseen hills behind Creetown.

Robert was already waiting for me at the street corner, torch in hand like a fellow-conspirator. Without any waste of time he set off away from the last of the houses. Over fences and ditches, down banks and across fields, through hedge-gaps and gates, he picked an unfaltering route, a route that in the pitch darkness had neither sequence nor meaning. It seemed quite strange to clear the last obstacle and step out at length on to the short crisp grass of the saltings.

From somewhere out of the blackness ahead came the "kleep, kleep, kleep" of oystercatchers taking off. On the edge

In the Crianlarich hills.
An Caisteal from Beinn Tulaichean

of a muddy runnel near-by an invisible golden plover piped at us mournfully.

After a couple of hundred yards Robert stopped and stood for a moment listening keenly. "That's them," he said quietly. "Can you hear them?"

But I heard nothing. The night still pressed in on us with the cold blank hostility of a dungeon wall. All I could do was to picture the geese on the unseen beach, congregated in their hundreds at the tide's edge, calling and clamouring as they waited impatiently to fly inland.

Then the darkness seemed to have lessened very slightly; so slightly that I was not sure if it was merely that my imagination was playing tricks. Anything would have been possible in this blank formless world, this queer void of no landmarks, no horizons, no sky. I was filled with admiration for the way in which Robert walked unerringly forward, avoiding the worst of the ditches and mud-holes, as unconcernedly as if we had been following Wigtown's main street.

"We'll wait here," he announced at last, dropping down into the ooze of a narrow creek. "They'll be coming over soon now; it's definitely getting lighter."

I followed him down the bank and tried to make myself comfortable on the shelving, sticky mud. The blackness round about was noticeably greyer. Occasionally now I could make out the excited talk of the geese down by the sea's edge.

Robert had timed things perfectly. We had no more than a few minutes to wait, barely long enough to become aware of the searching cold of the dawn wind.

At first the birds were scarcely visible, sensed rather than seen in the semi-darkness. They came in coveys of twos and threes, and the whirr of their wing-beats made a new kind of music on the wind. Gradually they became more numerous: some we could just make out gliding in no more than a score or so of yards away; others, farther off, were still completely invisible. Inescapably I became caught up in the surging excitement of this tremendous morning migration, this movement inland away from the tide-fringe to the sweetest grass of the saltings. In no more than two or three minutes the vast plain, bleak and barren, had become vibrant with life. Even my companion, seasoned campaigner as he was, had been infected by the sudden exhilaration. "Ackh, ackh!" he called, mimicking the greylags as they passed, hoping to call them down. "Ackh, ackh!" answered the birds, their great dark pinions beating past no more than a few feet above our heads.

On and on they came, more and more of them, still in occasional small groups though increasingly often in bigger skeins. And all the while the background sky grew steadily lighter.

"Here come the pinks!" exclaimed Robert, pointing suddenly seawards. "Just look at them; aren't they lovely?"

Catching the urgency in his voice, I swung round to watch. Low down they came, seeming at first almost to skim the bumps and banks of the saltings, heading straight towards us like a squadron of bombers in a fly-past. Then, as they neared, individual birds became distinguishable and I noted the faster wing-beats, the shriller note of their calling. They passed directly over our heads, swept round in a wide arc with magnificent precision, then dropped to land little more than a score of yards away.

"That was certainly worth seeing," I whispered, trying to keep my head well down behind the jagged lip of our creek. "Just look at the others, too, at their breakfast!"

There seemed indeed to be geese all round us, scattered in knots and clusters on ground that was scarcely more undulating than the first fairway at St. Andrews. The nearest of them were perhaps 15 yards away, those behind merging into the dim background of the saltings, while here and there sentinel ganders stood on guard, aloof and dignified, necks splendidly erect. I could appreciate now the expertness with which Robert had chosen our observation-post, for we were so close to the birds that we could even hear their feeding hum, that fascinating indication of supreme contentment which they give when they are at their grazing.

The goose [says Mrs. Lyn Irvine when telling of her own domestic flock] is the real artist among the grazing beasts, its movements with their tiny variations are so nimble. The noise is such that even the wind, hens cackling, a thrush singing, or a footstep on the turf is enough to drown it. But on a still evening one can hear the quick mandibles cropping the soft fresh herbage, a sound of extraordinary sweetness, a confidence from the heart of nature, a sound long-loved, like rain falling on trees after summer drought, like wind in the sheets of a boat.*

Our perception, of course, was hardly as finely tuned as that. Yet even in those few brief minutes we could not help catching something of the sheer grace and poetry around us. Here, in the very heart of this great concourse of the wild geese, was the climax of our waiting and watching, and we literally held our breath for fear of bringing it all to an end. I did my best to capture an indelible mental picture, regretting only that in the birds' plumage we had still to make do with monochrome rather than full colour, with silhouette and shadow rather than barred brown and lavender blue, ash-grey and pink and unflecked white.

Yet it would not be long before the growing daylight would bring colour everywhere. The ditches and runnels, mirroring the sky, had already begun to glint like silver; soon the grass itself would have lost all trace of its blank half-light pallor. Inevitably I thought of some of the other dawns Robert must have known, dawns much more full of pageantry than this one, when perhaps the sky burned like a furnace in defiance of oncoming rain, or when the packed snow, incredibly coloured by the sun, looked like the limitless wastes of Antarctica. Fortunately it had been obvious all along that, so far as his enthusiasm was concerned, the weather made not the least bit of difference.

Still the light increased, and still more geese kept arriving from the beaches. Clearly our good fortune could not be expected to last much longer.

"We've not much chance of deceiving the pinks," muttered Robert. "They're not fools, you know, not like the greylags. Just you wait and see. I don't think they'll like that black mackintosh of yours; it'll be something they didn't see here yesterday."

He was all too accurate in his forecast. Over our heads hurried another two or three gaggles of pinkfeet, still obviously without suspicion. Then suddenly, in a moment, everything was different. There was a violent swish of wings and the next line of oncoming birds shied aside as one. Equally swiftly their call-

---

* *Field with Geese*, by Lyn Irvine (Hamish Hamilton, 1960).

notes changed. There was no mistaking the warning, taken up and passed along the whole length of the skein. It was the same urgent message of alarm that we had heard that New Year's Day echoing over the waste of Gartrenich Moss.

I took off the offending coat and rolled it into an incon-spicuous-looking ball; then, to put it still further out of harm's way, I tried sitting on it in the glutinous ooze of mud. But the damage had been done. Geese give no second chances. Again and again now they swerved as they passed above us. We could even sense the restlessness which had come over those already feeding. Their hum had stopped, and now there was only uneasy silence.

We knew then that it was only a matter of time before fear would gain the mastery. Very obviously the restlessness grew. A few coveys took wing and melted away down wind. Still we could see plenty of birds round about us, heads up like stags in a corrie-bowl first scenting danger. But the nervousness was infectious and spread without check. More and more geese took off, formed up and unobtrusively disappeared, the thin black threads of their chevrons fine-drawn against the sky. There was no sudden panic, no wild confusion; the flight never became a rout. And yet, almost before we had properly appreciated it, we were alone. We stood up stiffly in our muddy hide-out and looked all round, across the bare grey-green turf. Not a goose was to be seen anywhere.

We walked over to the mud-banks flanking the estuary of the Bladnoch. A family of mallard splashed into untidy take-off as we approached and at the next kink in the river a huge flock of wigeon rose in a cloud to go on a quest for quieter territory elsewhere. But 'here was nothing now to tempt us to linger. We had become suddenly conscious of the icy cold, suddenly vulnerable to the shrivelling wind. We turned and re-crossed the saltings towards the hill and the village and our breakfasts, watched by a few aimlessly cruising gulls and a brazen pair of sheld-duck.

2

The Winter Seas

The winter day broke blue and bright,
With glancing sun and glancing spray,
As o'er the swell our boat made way,
As gallant as a gull in flight.

Wilfrid Wilson Gibson

IN the years closely following the visit to Wigtown Bay we were
to see the grey geese again many times: in Stirlingshire, in the
fields which flank the kinks and coils of the River Endrick; in
Kinross-shire, beside the misty expanse of Loch Leven; in
Perthshire, usually in the stubble-fields along the hollow of
Strath Earn.

In addition, however, my wife and I 'discovered' the
pleasures of visiting Islay in February; Islay, where the flocks
of wintering barnacle geese, amounting in some seasons to as
many as 10,000 birds, are believed to comprise about a sixth
of the world population. Two years running we made the
journey to the island for week-end stays, and so supremely
enjoyable did we find these that there has been a danger of
their becoming compulsive annual pilgrimages. The immense
concourses of barnacles in the fields or on the move to and
from their roosts beside Loch Gruinart, Loch Indaal and the
other sea-inlets are endlessly thrilling, while the lesser numbers
of greylags and white-fronts, and also the assortments of
wintering ducks and waders bring one to the conclusion that a
few 'stolen' days are not nearly enough.

There was, however, another reason for our visits to Islay
quite apart from the attractions of the geese. For long we had
heard that February, more than any other month in the year,
often provides the best weather for enjoyment of the Western
Isles. While the mainland is still shivering in the icy grasp of
winter, the Hebrides can be experiencing to the full the new
promise of spring: keen air, brilliant sunshine, far visibility,
with horizons pushed to the very rim of the world. We wanted

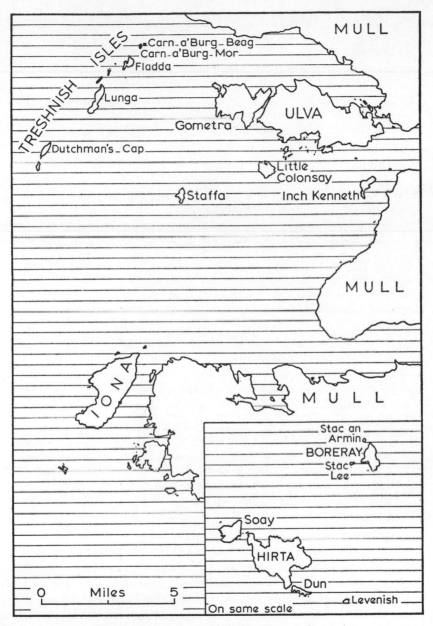

THE ISLANDS (inset the ST. KILDA GROUP)

to try out this theory for ourselves, to dispel the unbelief which made it so hard to credit. Fortunately our two week-ends, although by no means flawless, proved to our complete satisfaction just how right the contention had been.

They brought me indeed to the further conclusion that this was an aspect of the Highland year not nearly widely enough appreciated; that, with variations, it could be applied as a new—and vastly enjoyable—feature of the Scottish tourist calendar. In particular it could be recommended as a very simple and very effective tonic for the high-pressure business man working in the South, harassed, jaded and—certainly by well on in the winter—far beyond recalling anything worth mentioning of the previous summer's break.

It could all begin, for example, with the most exciting train in Britain: the train which every evening of the week except Saturday leaves King's Cross on its overnight run to Mallaig. And Mallaig in the depths of winter, as indeed in summer also, is the starting-point for one of the most interesting day-cruises on the whole of the West Coast of Scotland—round the Small Isles.

Take a leisurely taxi from office to station; eat an equally leisurely dinner as the train hustles north into Hertfordshire; then sleep the night through until the slower, less familiar rhythm of the curves of the West Highland line jogs you amiably awake somewhere beyond the upper reaches of Loch Lomond.

For the Scot, of course, the process is easier, though possibly rather less comfortable: the train is in Edinburgh between four and five in the morning and leaves Glasgow at six, so that it is necessary to be up before there is even the remotest hint of winter dawn. Thereafter, however, the rewards are equally handsome.

My own start was at Helensburgh, forty valuable minutes further on than Glasgow. It was a black starless morning, soft and damp, with the street-lamps blurring in a drifting haze of drizzle. As I walked to the station I felt lethargic and resentful; I also felt quite unbelievably stupid for embarking on an outing which seemed so certain to be a failure. Even breakfast, as we climbed through Glen Falloch round the unseen curve of the Dubh Eas viaduct and high above the scattering of pines down by the river, had a strange air of unreality. It was only at Bridge of Orchy that the first glimmers of daylight through the steamed-up carriage window began slowly to disclose the world outside; at that particular moment raw and bleak and unfriendly.

It was amusing to reflect how incredibly remote the lights of Leadenhall Street or Piccadilly would seem to our imaginary, half-awake London executive. Outside the haven of the compartment's warmth the pallid gleam of Loch Tulla; the old Wood of Crannach, snow-carpeted, the gnarled branches of its pines grotesquely outstretched; then Rannoch Muir itself, with the mist low over the limitless acres of white-dusted heather, its lochans frozen, its sluggish river-curves desolate as those of central Iceland; and again and again beyond the dilapidated drift-fences the silhouettes of stags, grazing or roaming away on another of their patient hunger-prompted quests. The contrast was bizarre to say the least.

How different too a frosty dawn would have been! The sun coming up behind the hills round Loch Ossian and far back to Ben Alder; furnace-light flaring across the moor; snow sparkling blue and gold and crimson. Views as unfamiliar to the summer visitor as ice-shows at the South Pole and already infinitely worth that all-night journey from London.

Beyond the Moor and Loch Treig and the first black pools of the Spean gorges it was the winter birches which caught my eye—every tree bare of leaves but hung with millions of raindrops in a haze of purple-blue. Then we were clattering into Fort William, eager for the interlude of the morning papers before the further run to Mallaig.

For years now there has existed the threat of the greatest misfortune in British railway history—the closure of the line between Fort William and Mallaig. Indeed with a relatively high subsidy in force, it may well be that by the time these words are first read the threat will have become sorry fact.

The Mallaig section of the West Highland Railway was built between January 1897 and March 1901, after a storm of political wrangling. Forty miles long, it was provided with seven intermediate stations and a private halt at Beasdale; bridges and viaducts—the most spectacular that at Glenfinnan, with twenty-one spans—were built of concrete, a novelty in those days; the tunnels, originally expected to number two, finally totalled eleven, while no less than 100 cuttings had to be excavated. It was no small feat of railway engineering, yet of inestimable advantage to the local inhabitants, whose previous travel facilities had amounted to a single horse-drawn stage-coach running three days a week in each direction between Arisaig and Fort William and taking seven and a half hours for the single journey.

From Banavie and Corpach at the south-western end of the Caledonian Canal the line follows the shore of Loch Eil then climbs to the watershed above Glenfinnan and the head of Loch Shiel; on the farther side it drops again to the western seaboard to link Lochailort, Arisaig, Morar and Mallaig. Without any question it is the most beautiful stretch of railway in the world: its views—down Loch Shiel, alongside Loch Eilt, over Loch nam Uamh, and out to the islands of Eigg, Rum and Skye beyond the white sands of Morar—are unsurpassed in the West Highlands; if there are colours more magical anywhere I have yet to hear tell of them. And almost without exception, as the train snakes round the most impossibly unexpected bends, every glimpse is seen to much greater advantage than from the more prosaic levels of the road below. Every mile has its history, romantic and tragic. Why this relatively short section of line has never been utilised as one of the finest strands in the whole Scottish tourist network— with coaches as clean and comfortable as those of Switzerland, with tempting eating facilities and with genuinely first-class overnight accommodation in Fort William and Mallaig— passes comprehension. What in fact has happened? The stations have been allowed to rust and rot in decay—might this perhaps have been deliberate policy so that the value of the line could be underplayed and its closure hastened? No special facilities for tourists have been provided, in fact even the former summer observation car has long since been withdrawn. Every effort, it would seem, has been made to create the impression that the section is down, out and finished.

Everywhere in summer the views are superb, especially when the heather is at its best; as I saw them, not so long after Christmas, they were literally breathtaking. Down by Loch Eilt especially, where the water was mirror-calm, the browns of the moor-grass, the greys of the rock-bluffs and the silver of burns and snow made unforgettable reflection-sequences among the islet pines. Then suddenly out to the west there was that first glimpse of Eigg, the Sgurr black as a battle-cruiser's prow, and, beyond, the peaks of Rum, ridge and top and corrie white with a powdering of snow, flashing in an unexpected promise of sunshine.

At first Mallaig pier seemed a cheerless exchange for the hothouse comfort of the railway compartment. The north wind came bustling round sheds and stacks of goods and waiting lorries with a touch that could hardly be described as friendly. Even the inevitable rows of herring-gulls gave the impression of huddling disconsolately against its malice.

Then I was being greeted by Mr. Livingstone, MacBrayne's manager, and suddenly Mallaig's welcome seemed very different. With him I watched the *Loch Seaforth* embarking her passengers and final cargo before leaving for Portree and Stornoway; then the *Loch Arkaig*, which had been lying off, moved alongside to tie up in her place and I was introduced to her master, Captain Kennedy. By this time the sun was making a more determined effort to come out; there was an encouraging sparkle to the sea; even the gulls had become more lively and across the bay there were the cormorants to watch. I went aboard and managed to find a corner on deck out of the wind; it was warm enough to imagine it was actually enjoyable sitting out for my brief bread and cheese lunch.

Between whiles it was amusing to reflect on what sort of feelings the imaginary London executive would have been having all this time if he had been in my shoes. Mixed, of course: deciding one moment maybe that he was every kind of a fool for hanging about on a draughty open deck, bound some time or other for nowhere and trying, with oldish Mallaig rolls and un-dainty hunks of cheddar, to stop his teeth from chattering. But then his gaze would start wandering—out to Eigg, to the snow-rimmed corries of Rum, to the Cuillin Ridge on Skye, every top and edge from Gars-Bheinn to the pinnacles of Sgurr nan Gillean chiselled against pale luminous blue. He might even come to the conclusion that it was worth it.

At last, formalities ashore completed, Captain Kennedy came aboard and the gangway was withdrawn. A few moments later the engine-room telegraph was jangling and we were away. It was 1.20 p.m. Quickly we picked up speed. Black skerries and cormorants fell astern as the *Loch Arkaig* cut a tossing white swathe in the cold gunmetal of the sea. Behind, the confusion of drifting mist and snow-ridges broadened out into the background of the mainland hills.

There were seven passengers on board the *Loch Arkaig* apart from myself. "Quite a busy day really," Captain Kennedy told me later. "In summer," he added, "we've occasionally had up to 160, but at this time of the year we can run out to Canna without any passengers at all and with no more than a handful of mail. Then, of course, the call at Muck is suspended during the winter; the harbour there is decidedly tricky. The islanders just have to rely on the service via Eigg."

Maintaining obscure winter schedules such as this to the Small Isles, day in day out, often enough with next to no passengers and in the most hostile weather conditions, has been an essential part of the MacBrayne service all down the years. The off-season pattern indeed is just as much a part of the overall picture as is the more familiar one of summer. Small wonder it is that high subsidies and rising freight rates have had to be the rule and not the exception. Yet it is an aspect of the islands' economy that is sometimes conveniently ignored by not a few fiery critics of MacBrayne's.

Returning home to Galmisdale, on Eigg, was Mr. Fergus Gowans, an Inverness county councillor. Talking with him, I learned disheartening details of the decline in the Small Isles' resident population. When he first went to live on Eigg in 1947, the population was about 110; today it is 53. On Muck it is 22, Rum 42 and Canna 23. Tragic figures indeed.

Just how desperately the numbers have fallen may be judged from the corresponding figures in the *Statistical Account* of 1796: Eigg 399, Muck 193, Rum 443 and Canna 304; and even these were already trending downwards. "In the years 1788 and 1790," says the *Account*, "183 souls emigrated from this parish to America and 55 to the mainland of Scotland and to neighbouring islands; of these 176 left Eigg." Reasons are not far to seek, for it is recorded how the islanders lived chiefly on potatoes and herrings, their greatest luxuries being "a dish of tea and a dram of whisky".

Of all the four islands Rum at present seems to hold out the brightest hope for the future. Thanks to the fact that it is under the jurisdiction of the Nature Conservancy, life there is much more stable. There are now twenty-one children on the island, whereas there are only eight on Eigg, five on Muck and five on Canna. In 1796 there were altogether 327 children under the age of 10 on the four islands.

It was a disappointment to me that the *Loch Arkaig* was not to be calling at the smallest of the Small Isles, Muck, for although I had seen it fairly often in the distance—for example from Sanna Bay near Ardnamurchan Point and from the splendid summit viewpoint of the Sgurr of Eigg—I had never actually been there. It is in fact an island that is relatively rarely visited, especially as, for yachtsmen, it is uncomfortably close to the wild seas off Ardnamurchan, and the reefs which defend it rule out any safe anchorage.

In Gaelic *muc* means 'pig' or 'sow', so that Eilean nam Muc is the 'island of swine'—Swynes Ile indeed is what Sir Donald Monro called it back in the sixteenth century. Even in those days it had the reputation of being particularly fertile, so kindly is it treated by the moist Atlantic climate, and today, like Canna, it can grow what are possibly the earliest potatoes in Scotland.

The meaning of the name Eigg is 'notch' or 'hollow' and, true to this, the formation of the island is that of a double wedge down-tilted to a central valley. The northern half is finely cliff-girt, the southern dominated by the immense dark tower of the Sgurr, which seems to rise to a far greater height than its modest 1,289 feet.

As we made in towards the shelter of the Eigg anchorage, Galmisdale Bay, I could not help thinking of the sea-birds we would have seen had it been the height of the breeding season: guillemots, black guillemots (or tysties, to give them their Northern name), razorbills and, most interesting of all, many companies of the Manx shearwaters which every summer nest in their burrows high up on the cliff-edges. Perhaps, too, we might have seen a few gannets, or solan geese, at their fishing, though times have changed completely since Monro's day, in 1549, when he could write of both Eigg and Rum as having "mony solenne geis". It would in any event have been a busy, exhilarating sight. Now everything was at its quietest: only a small number of gulls and occasional distant glimpses of what were perhaps tysties in their unfamiliar winter colouring, which has much more white about it than in summer.

We stopped for twenty minutes off Galmisdale while the scarlet ferryboat edged alongside and cargoes were exchanged with much Gaelic banter and no obvious sense of urgency. Then Mr. Gowans and a family of four climbed aboard; in a few moments they were away, heading shorewards. It all made a superb artist's picture, the red small-boat dazzlingly high-lighted by the afternoon winter sun against the laughing browns of the moors and, over all, the huge chocolate battle-ments of the Sgurr.

The wind was in our faces, ice-cold and exhilarating, as the *Loch Arkaig* turned away and headed up the steep east side of Eigg. Through the island's notch the rock-spire of Trallval, on Rum, stood clear like the tip of a Chamonix *aiguille*. We were holding a course remarkably close inshore, so that in the keen visibility every boulder and gully was distinct. Sgurr nan h'Iolaire, 'peak of the eagles', dropped astern and with it the white waterfall-threads which must look strikingly impressive in times of heavy spate. This part of the island—unlike the arc of cliffs behind Cleadale on the western side and, of course, the Sgurr itself—has still to yield any rock-climbing routes of interest. The cliff-faces, which mark an old coastline and are now actually some distance inland, are steep and rise in places as high as 500 feet, but they are reported to be broken up too frequently by grassy terraces. Doubtless all the same some enthusiast of the future will come along and accomplish some near-impossible climbing feat just to prove that present verdicts are wrong.

With the afternoon sun now low, we were in shadow as the *Loch Arkaig* skirted the north-eastern nose of the island. Then suddenly as we swung a few points westwards we were caught in daylight once more. The whole Sound of Rum stretched out like a flood of gold, beyond it those familiar island hills with the Viking names, Ashval, Askival, Allival; almost 20 miles to starboard, behind Loch Scavaig and the humble island out-line of Soay, the snow-silver of the Cuillin provided an impres-sive counter-attraction. Birds were few, but once a razorbill came whirring overhead, circling uncharacteristically as if to make quite sure it had been positively identified.

Looking up at the shapely wedge of Askival (2,659 feet), highest peak on Rum and possibly the finest-shaped mountain in Scotland apart from Skye, I smiled to think back to the May morning sixteen years before when last I had sampled its delights. Theo Nicholson and I had been camping by the shore of Loch Scresort, the sea-loch which makes such a spacious, sheltered anchorage on the east side of Rum. We had stayed for a superlative heat-wave week-end, making a round of the complete 'Ridge' the highlight of our visit. Then, after sufficient time to recover some of our energy, we had scrambled once again to the summit of Askival by its steep eastern ridge, determined not to miss a final hour or two of enjoyment before we left. It was only 9 a.m. when we reached the cairn, but already the morning heat had achieved a brazen ferocity that was reflected back by every rock we touched. There was only one thing to be desired more than anything else in the world—a long, cool bathe. We found the answer in a delectable little tarn, Lochan Coire nan Grunnd, cupped in parched moorland below the Askival-Allival ridge. We went in, I remember, off a sun-baked heather bank and floated in the most satisfying luxury imaginable, looking back to the steps and stairs we had climbed, already withdrawn and remote in the heat-haze.

By the time the *Loch Arkaig* had swung between the sheltering arms of Loch Scresort the sun was hidden once more behind the hills; the winter shadows had flowed like a tide across the whole amphitheatre of the bare, enclosing moors. Scanning the shore-line above the seaweed and lichen-yellow rocks, I tried to decide just where Theo and I had chosen our summer camp-site, but without success: it all looked coldly inhospitable, surely not the place where we had fought a running battle with hordes of local clegs and crept into the tent to escape the burning glare of the sun.

Small rafts of eiders moved quietly aside as we headed up the centre of the loch and slowed down to meet the island ferryboat which came out to meet us. One of our remaining passengers transferred to the ferry, muffled to the ears in his duffle-coat. He was followed by crate after crate of canned beer —enough, I decided, to ensure that the local population would survive for a little while longer without undue hardship; in their place we took on board three rather skinny-looking bags of mail. Then once again, as the small-boat cast off, the engine telegraph was ringing. A cheery exchange of waves and the *Loch Arkaig* began to pick up speed. For the islanders another day's call was over.

It was in 1957 that Rum was declared one of the National Nature Reserves of Scotland. Its 26,400 acres—100 of which are woodland—provide the Nature Conservancy with an area of exceptional interest for geological and botanical research, while it is now the principal centre in Britain for the study of red deer. At the time when the new régime began, some 1,700 sheep which shared the grazing with the 1,600 deer were taken off, thus allowing full scope for intensive studies not only of population, but of numerous other questions which were never previously given the attention they deserved.

I was just about to try and identify an interesting-looking bird near the mouth of the loch—a great northern diver maybe —when Captain Kennedy invited me to join him in the wheel-house. The invitation was thoroughly welcome and I was not slow to take the opportunity of escaping from the chill of the open deck.

"This next stretch out to Canna," commented the Captain, "is apt to be the worst of the whole round. Especially in a north-westerly gale. Today it's more of a westerly swell; not bad at all, though you can tell there's been some dirty weather farther out." The slow rhythm of heave and lift seemed moderate enough; it was left to the imagination to picture the fury of an insane nor' wester piling into the funnel of the Cuillin Sound, between Skye and the Small Isles, from the exposed waters of the Sea of the Hebrides.

The *Loch Arkaig*, I learned, had been on the Small Isles run for six years, having previously been serving the island of Raasay from Kyle of Lochalsh and Portree. With her speed of 11 knots she is capable of operating in anything up to a Force 8 gale; above that, especially if the wind is from an awkward quarter, conditions are liable to be impossible. It sometimes happens that the final outward 'leg' across the Sound of Canna just cannot be risked at all and a return has to be made direct to Mallaig. Great store apparently is set on the weather fore-

February sunshine.
The view north-eastwards from Beinn Chabhair

casts for shipping, while shore-contact is always available if necessary by radio-telephone with Oban.

As we rounded the northernmost tip of Rum, the hills of South Uist, Beinn Mhor and Hecla, came into view almost 40 miles away to the west. Then it was Canna itself which took up our attention, the black mass of Compass Hill, like some huge ungainly sea-monster, a bulky contrast to the slim sea-stack of Bod an Stoil, the Pillar Rock, at its base.

For nearly three centuries Compass Hill has been notorious for the magnetic influence of the iron in its basaltic rocks. When he visited the Western Isles in 1695 Martin Martin wrote of Canna: "There is a high hill in the north end, which disorders the needle in the compass: I laid the compass on the stony ground near it, and the needle went often round with great swiftness, and instead of settling towards the north, as usual, it settled here due east. The stones in the surface of the earth are black, and the rock below facing the sea is red; some affirm that the needle of a ship's compass, sailing by the hill, is disordered by the force of the magnet in this rock: but of this I have no certainty." The phenomenon has been considered of sufficient importance to be given mention in the Admiralty "Sailing Directions".

Through the gap to the left of Canna we could just distinguish a minute needle a dozen miles off: the lighthouse on the lonely islet cluster of Hyskeir, where, on the shelving pitchstone rocks, there is a small colony of grey seals. As we watched, the first swift flashes of the light itself winked through the growing dusk.

Often enough in the past I had looked out to Canna from the eaves and gutters of the Cuillin Ridge; occasionally too I had been able to make out the faint pencil-dot of Hyskeir, notably from Allival and Askival on Rum. But this was the first time I had had the good fortune actually to sail out to the western edge of the Small Isles and I looked forward keenly to making closer acquaintance with Canna.

We seemed to make the 6-mile approach from the northern tip of Rum with surprising slowness. The sun was down now and it was becoming steadily more difficult to decide on details in the silhouettes ahead. Then, quite suddenly, we were running into the harbour, the sheltering barrier of Sanday island

Approaching St. Kilda.
Hirta, Boreray and Stac an Armin

momentarily as the diesels went into reverse, then edged gently
in to the pier, landing lights switched on.

Captain Kennedy moved in from his point of vantage overlooking the gangway, his hand no longer nursing the telegraph.
"That's that," he commented quietly. "It's always a problem
coming in to the pier here at low tide as it is now. I wouldn't
like to say how far we're off the bottom—not far anyway."
Certainly the thick mass of seaweed-fronds, writhing along the
rocks like huge black congers, looked ready enough to hold us
fast in their clutches.

The western end of Sanday is joined to Canna at low water
so that between them the two islands form a small but well-
sheltered haven, especially welcome when a south-westerly gale
is blowing up. Here in times of storm innumerable fishing-
boats and other small craft have found sanctuary. Over the
years a favourite ploy of the fishermen has been to decorate
the wall of rock behind the pier with the names of their
boats and home ports, and it was interesting to read these,
the white lettering still standing out clearly in the fading
light.

Canna in storm must be vulnerable indeed, when winter
gales make wild music on the hill-slopes which rise bleak and
bare to almost 700 feet, or rush mercilessly through the low
central gap at Tarbert. But in the serene blue days of early
summer, with long views to the peaks of Skye and Rum, it must
have an idyllic charm that would be difficult to surpass
anywhere. Its north-facing cliffs are reputedly of interest for
their sea-bird colonies—especially as the island, like Eigg and
Rum, is a station for the Manx shearwater—and when the sea
is calm under a hot June sun it must be fascinating to take a
small-boat on a voyage of exploration among its flanking stacks
and skerries.

It was nearly six o'clock when the ropes were cast off once
more and the *Loch Arkaig* reversed slowly away into the darkness. During the half-hour call a good deal of cargo had been
off-loaded, watched by what looked like the entire population
of Canna. Last of the out-going passengers, the laird himself
had gone ashore and in his stead a young priest had embarked
for the run back to Mallaig.

I was tempted to go below for a welcome bowl of soup in the warmth of the diminutive saloon. It seemed wrong, however, to miss any possible enjoyment on deck and I was soon back at my vantage-point in the lee of the ship's squat little funnel. Canna was still a bulky mass beyond the froth of the *Loch Arkaig*'s wake, but growing less distinct now against the last faint bars of the sunset. The fixed light on Sanday shone out cheerily, as though reluctant to let us away, but the more powerful flashes of Hyskeir lighthouse were still hidden by an intervening headland.

An hour later I took one more, final turn on deck. The wind had fallen away but the cold was even more intense and exhilarating beyond description. The stars were out in an incomparable profusion, their brilliance barely impaired by the half moon which linked us in a roadway of silver with the black cliffs of Eigg. Only to the north did there seem to be any trace of cloud, a thin white cap trailing over the Cuillin—and it might well have been snow. No one was about; momentarily I had the sensation of being utterly alone in space. Only the radar scanner turning purposefully above the wheelhouse seemed a link with the world of reality.

It was 8.15 when, at length, the *Loch Arkaig* swung round and slowed at Mallaig pier, edging gently into a confusion of brilliant light and pools of black darkness. No one seemed particularly interested in the final act of what, after all, had been nothing more than an ordinary routine round. Yet as I said good-night to Captain Kennedy and stepped rather stiffly ashore, I knew that for me at least this had been no ordinary day.

I spent the night in hotel comfort in Mallaig, then caught the south-bound train the following morning and was home in Helensburgh for lunch. For the London executive the end of it all could well have been spun out more pleasurably still, with a leisurely morning in Mallaig and then, once again, the enjoyment of the West Highland line and the sleeper journey home. It would be surprising to say the least if, after that, the office desk did not seem just a little more tolerable, the way ahead a fraction clearer for a touch of Hebridean perspective.

3

The Ridges

It is in quietness on the hills that we listen best.

F. S. Smythe

THE shattering explosion of the alarm-clock jarred me brutally awake. It was 5.30 a.m., still long enough before the February dawn would break. Beyond the comforting defence of the bedclothes, I sensed the hostility of the frost and the darkness.

It was a morning which belonged to those halcyon days of the past when Inverarnan Hotel was still open all the year round, with that reputation for hospitality which was to become almost legendary in the world of climbers and skiers. I had arrived there the previous evening, to be given the customary cheery welcome and every help in arranging for a quick getaway in the morning. Now, facing the battle of dressing and solitary breakfast, it was not so easy to avoid seeing more than a hint of folly in the whole uncomfortable proceeding.

Outside on the road the ice-jab of the air fairly knocked the breath from me; it seemed almost like the douche of a suddenly breaking wave. It was still moonlight and so quiet that it was as if the world itself was reluctant to stir into wakefulness. Even the River Falloch was muted. I paused for a few moments on the bridge which crosses over to Beinn Ghlas farm. Almost directly underneath, a broad pool made a mirror which caught the moonlight and reflected in detail the silvered slopes of the hills. There was no wind; not a ripple of current distorted the picture. It was one of those rare, unforgettable glimpses which sometimes, quite unexpectedly, go towards the compensation of discomfort.

I was bound for the Crianlarich hills, for the long friendly ridge that swings through 10 miles of switchbacks from Beinn Chabhair in the south-west to the twin summits of Stobinian and Ben More. Thanks to the Alpine start, the whole of the February day stretched ahead, but how far it would be possible to get, how many miles and thousands of feet of climbing would prove to be a fair ration, remained to be seen as the hours wore on. Meanwhile the hardest work of the day was just beginning.

Beyond the farm steading, on the east side of the Falloch, the hill-slopes lift fiercely for 750 feet. There is a suggestion of a path through the birches and boulders and mat of bracken, but, only faintly visible, it was of no great help. The stars, however, had begun to pale and the light was increasing sufficiently to reduce the chances of cracking a shin. Every now and again my attention was diverted by the ice-display on the familiar falls which spill down giant steps to the glen. The burn itself was not completely frozen over, but its violence had been curbed and along its edges wafers and crusts of ice, in an endless variety of patterns, decorated each angle and overhang.

Higher up it was the dawn lighting which brought me to a halt. I had grunted and grumbled my way up the worst of the introductory slopes, thankful that at last the tangle of vegetation had begun to thin. Then I happened to look back. Beyond the black trench of the glen and the head of Loch Lomond, the corrie of Ben Vorlich and, northwards, the wedge of Beinn Laoigh were catching the first rays of the sun. A soft pink blush, indescribably beautiful, had suffused their snows and, as I watched, it spread slowly downwards in a gentle tide. Rock-ribs made black edgings; above, the sky's luminous blue was gradually deepening. The most delicate colouring lasted no more than a few minutes, for the daylight was rapidly becoming more harsh. But even so it was a transformation that put me in mind inevitably of half-forgotten dawns in the Alps, those brief moments at the start of an expedition when the glacier lanterns go out and, all round, the peaks give promise of another long day of sunshine.

The first objective on my ridge-walk was Beinn Chabhair (3,053 feet), said rather oddly to mean 'mountain of the antler'. Two of its three ridges—the south-west and the north-east—lie on the watershed of Scotland, the burns on the one side flowing eventually to the Forth and the North Sea, and on the other to Loch Lomond and the Firth of Clyde. For much of the day the route would actually lie along this watershed line.

It was a relief to reach little Lochan Beinn Chabhair, half-way stage on the western approaches. It came as a thoroughly welcome break, for the ground which leads up to it once the brow of the first slopes has been passed is a desert of knolls and peat-hags, rising only slightly in height. The monotony makes one realise all too forcefully how far back from the road Beinn Chabhair lies and why visitors tend to be rarer here than else-where on the Crianlarich hills.

The lochan itself, with its unexpected boathouse, puts an end to the tedium. It is cupped by the third of Beinn Chabhair's ridges, the western, which swings up in ribs and spines like a monstrous dorsal fin, and the escape up the face of this to the summit is very much steeper. Here, if anywhere, is the kind of place C. E. Montague doubtless had in mind when he pictured "what it is like when the contour lines begin to sing together, like the Biblical stars".

For 1,400 feet a succession of scoops and gullies, walled by rock outcrops, led upwards. There was fine firm snow under-foot, so that there was no trouble in treading a pleasant staircase all the way to the ridge. A dozen yards away, spilling snow-icing down its sides like a hurriedly finished Christmas cake, stood the first cairn of the day.

Up to this point I believe I had scarcely noticed the sun-shine. Now, suddenly, I realised how it had increased in power. In all directions it flashed on friendly peaks, deep in snow, under a sky still unflecked with cloud. From the ice-jewelling on the cairn at my elbow the way ahead stretched in a gradually climbing avenue of white to the distant, beckoning crests of Ben More and Stobinian.

The only snag was the wind. Completely harmless though it was, its icy touch was a reminder that this was, after all, a morning in February and no more than breakfast-time at that. I soon took the hint, therefore, and started off again downhill.

Beinn Chabhair's eastern face drops 1,000 feet to the An Caisteal col. I cast around hopefully for some suitably inclined gully down which to glissade, but the snow was hard-frozen and demanded a certain amount of respect, so my search was in vain. Perhaps it was as well. I contented myself instead with the more normal rate of descent which I adopt when on my own among the winter hills—a progression which is the epitome of caution. No doubt the occasional peck with the axe, when the crust was particularly hard, made me look more than usually like an elderly hen scratching in a back-yard.

Arriving at the bealach, I sat down for a few moments, reflecting somewhat ruefully on the amount of valuable sweat-won height that the descent had cost me. It would all have to be regained, plus an additional 200 feet, before the next summit was reached.

Although frost still held the mastery, the sun was continuing to gain in power; the indigo shadows it cast were steadily decreasing in length. I looked down the 3-mile umber smudge of the Allt a' Chuilinn to where it joined the Falloch. There was no movement or sign of life to be seen on the main road beyond, but it was not difficult to picture the ski-burdened cars hurrying north, already well on their way to Glencoe or Ben Lawers. Even on this February morning the traffic which there would be later on in the day seemed to typify all the stir and noise and irritation nowadays accepted as normal. Complete solitude, even for a little while, was infinitely worth the effort it had demanded.

The next goal was a glistening white snow-dome set against a sky of brilliant, Alpine blue.

An Caisteal, 'the castle' (3,265 feet), was no new hill for me. But I had known it and thought of it as green and lush with summer vegetation, rather a sultry, wearisome ascent by one or other of the twin ridges it sends down northwards to Glen Falloch. Now, in the tonic air of this winter morning, it could scarcely have been more different. The snow was impeccably white, the sun almost hot on my back. There was no need to hurry—indeed I wanted only to spin out the exhilarating mixture of warmth and biting cold for as long as possible; it was good to feel, even momentarily, that one was treading some high stairway in the Valais or the Oberland rather than (with all due respect to it) a humble Perthshire 'Munro'. Even the wind gave no trouble till near the ridge, then, as I trod the last yards to the cairn, it came storming over from the north in gusts which sent the loose snow whirling like spindrift.

The time was now 10.20 a.m. Thus far I had been moving well to schedule. With two summits attained, I felt thoroughly

satisfied and was able to enjoy fully the wider range of views
that had opened out to the west: Beinn Buidhe, at the head of
Loch Fyne; the white ridges of Cruachan, and in between—a
hazy blur on the horizon over 50 miles away—Ben More in
Mull. And what a day this would have been for climbing Ben
More! I pictured the last few hundred feet of its magnificent
north-east ridge, eaves and cornices of snow far out-thrust over
the corrie, a foreground to the blue of Loch na Keal and all the
pattern of islands from Eorsa and Ulva and Little Colonsay to
the outer barrier screen of the Treshnish Isles. A tremendous
prospect; but then, what hill in the whole of Scotland would
not be giving of its best on a morning such as this?

Next objective was Beinn a' Chroin, according to the guide-
book, 'the mountain of the cloven hoof'. Just how this hill
should have come by such a name is rather difficult to under-
stand. There is nothing obviously Satanic about it and even in
shape it is very ordinary looking, with a level wedge of a ridge
half a mile long linking two tops of 3,104 feet and 3,078 feet.
Perhaps the name resulted from one of those flashes of inspiration which every now and again prompted the Gael to go in for
something a little different from his usual run of big hills and
black hills, red hills and rough hills; something exotic like
'the smallpox peak' he conjured up in Skye, or 'the cairn of the
basket' in the Monadh Liath, or even that masterpiece of
humour up in Glen Shiel, 'the whelk'. The only other explana-
tion would seem to be that whoever tried to find a meaning for
the name allowed his own imagination to have a little harmless
fun.

Quite a steep wall confronts the climber as he approaches
Beinn a' Chroin from the An Caisteal col. It is not a place of
any difficulty, but in winter when the sunless cracks and corners
become plated with ice and give the defences a more formidable
appearance than usual, it is as well to treat it with respect. A
slanting terrace where a few steps had to be slashed in the
snow-ice took me quickly upwards and landed me eventually
at the west end of the summit wedge. Thence the half-mile
crest which leads to the higher, eastern top is not nearly so level
as it looks from a distance. It is in fact a switchback of many
tiresome bumps. The wind kept pushing and bullying me all
the way along it, except where it was possible to sneak aside to

the sun-warmed lee-slopes, and I was not at all sorry to reach the cairn and yet another drop beyond.

My only previous visit to this top had been with my brother Colin on 31st December 1937. Although the last day of the year, it had been so warm that we were able to climb stripped to the waist. Our approach had been from the youth hostel at Monachylemore, and we had had a memorable insight into the heart of Balquhidder. From Beinn a' Chroin we had travelled fast over Beinn Tulaichean and Cruach Ardrain, yet even with all our hustling, dusk was changing swiftly to darkness as we dropped down the north shoulder of Stob Garbh to Crianlarich and the bringing in of the New Year.

These eastern approaches by the Braes of Balquhidder are less well known than those on the Glen Falloch side of the hills; yet at every season of the year they repay fully any attention that is given them.

The 'Country of Broken Men' the Braes are sometimes called, for long ago in their fastnesses Rob Roy and many another in the same line of business sought safe sanctuary from the law. Yet nowadays as one follows the shore-lines of Loch Voil and Loch Doine, only peace and quiet are to be found. It is no motorway that runs the 8 miles westward from Kingshouse to Inverlochlarig, but a road old-fashioned in character, with a profusion of bumps and bends, blind corners and short sharp gradients. Travel it on foot when the ground is iron hard and the bordering carpet of dead leaves is dusted with rime; or drive along it on an evening of early summer, when the green of the trees still has its freshness, when swallows are busy round the steadings and redstarts or maybe an occasional bullfinch may be seen escaping into the hedges. A scattering of buildings marks the road-end at Inverlochlarig, and the complex network of farm tracks unravels only as one climbs to the ridges beyond. Indeed, the differences from Glen Falloch make the whole cirque of hills from Stobinian southwards seem like a completely strange bit of country; and yet, to gain this new familiarity is always wholly worth while.

From high on the snows of Beinn a' Chroin it was difficult to picture summer in Balquhidder. In the long glen there was no green, only brown and smoky blue; far below the ridge-crest the lowest of the drifts poked white fingers into the rust of dead moorland. However, down in the dip to Beinn Tulaichean, 3,099 feet and the next of the day's summits, there was a rocky niche; even from a distance it was obvious that it had been designed by nature for lunch and a siesta. To it I willingly turned. Sheltered from the wind, I basked in the midday sun for a full forty minutes and wolfed some badly needed sandwiches. With the least further encouragement I would have got my head down properly and continued the sleep that had been so rudely interrupted seven hours before.

Even this self-indulgence cost me dear. It was an effort to heave myself to my feet again and start yet another upward grind. Hard work had lost its savour. The rot had begun to set in.

As I started up the 1,600 feet to Beinn Tulaichean, the tiredness which at once beset me was both physical and mental. The ground round the saddle was featureless uninspiring desert and escape from it seemed to take an inordinately long time. It had become a struggle to lift one foot above the other, and as step succeeded step I found myself moving more and more slowly. I tried counting, but that was boring too; over and over again, endlessly, step followed step. Fancy suggested condemnation to a treadmill, for the route lay up a broad and steepening face, always much less exhilarating than a ridge. The heat and the glare, untempered here by any wind, seemed to have shrivelled all enthusiasm. Even the snow, which in the early sunshine had flashed fire and colour, appeared to mock my snail's pace with an unrelieved monotony.

It was a relief—seemingly an eternity later—to reach the skyline edge. Here the renewed touch of the breeze was as refreshing as an iced drink, the view a new encouragement to carry on. The contrast with the restriction of the lower slopes of being able to look now from Badenoch to the Sleeping Warrior, in Arran, now from Mull or the wedge of Ben Starav to the ice-chiselling of Ben Lomond's northern corrie, made all the difference to the last 250 feet. If Beinn Tulaichean, 'the knolly hill', had begun as drudgery, at least its final word had been an inspiration.

On the further climb up Cruach Ardrain, which involved another 700 feet of ascent, there was even more to whip the last ounces of effort from my flagging pace. For one thing, the slope

was set at just the right angle—not too steep, not too gentle—
and it was vastly encouraging to see how quickly the promontory which runs out to Beinn Tulaichean was beginning to drop
behind and below. For another, the snow was once again of that
ideal consistency which is such a joy to tread, firm and compact,
with no suggestion of any sogginess or, worse still, of unreliable
crust. It was a ridge I was climbing now, a stairway of curves
and domes, fluted, sculptured, moulded by the wind into an
infinite variety of patterns. Even the monotony of colouring
had gone, with cream and gold alternating with the indigo
shadows against the background sky.

Cruach Ardrain (3,428 feet) deserves much kindlier treat-
ment from the translators than 'the big heap', for it is a fine
mountain, magnificently proportioned, identifiable from afar
and possessing too much character of its own to be in any way
overawed by its mighty neighbours, Ben More and Stobinian.
Whether visited in autumn, when, sometimes, the new snow is
blown streaming from its narrow top like an Everest plume, or
in early spring when frost binds the steep slopes iron hard, it
is one Scottish hill that is never easily forgotten. In addition, it
offers one of the most enjoyable winter routes hereabouts—the
well-known Y-Gully, which cleaves the north face for some
hundreds of feet. As I made my way upwards, I was interested to
see a party of three climbers appear at the cairn, then turn to
descend in my direction. I guessed that they had been in the
gully, and this duly proved to be so, for they described how
they had had a fine climb with some long bouts of step-cutting.
Later I watched them enjoying a fast glissade valleywards from
above the Grey Height.

The rest of the story is soon told. From Cruach Ardrain I
looked across to Stobinian and Ben More, the last two summits
of the Crianlarich group—and the highest—and as I did so I
knew once and for all that I would not be treading their tops
that day. In the pool of afternoon shadow the gulf between
looked thoroughly uninviting. The long, long descent would
have to be followed by a re-ascent to Stobinian of almost
2,200 feet and on top of that again there would still be the
parabola between it and Ben More, 1,000 feet deep. The spirit
might be reasonably willing, but the flesh was woefully weak for
facing a last dragging crawl of this kind, a crawl that would

bring the day's total to over 10,000 feet of ascent. And to cap everything, the final descent of Ben More—alone, tired and in gathering darkness, on slopes that would be iced once the sun was off them—might perhaps have been said to be lacking in prudence.

There was more comfort to say the least in thinking long thoughts of the bath and dinner that awaited me, not so far off now, at Crianlarich.

Any last lingering doubts I may have had were quickly banished on the little subsidiary top of Cruach Ardrain, Stob Garbh. The descent to the intervening saddle and short further climb along its spine were wretchedly laborious and each ten feet of snow-plastered rock and scree felt like a hundred. I was profoundly thankful to flop down at last beside the cairn and admit that the drudgery of the day was done.

I fished out a bar of chocolate, rather the worse for wear, from the depths of my rucksack and relaxed, back against grey rock. All around the shadows had begun to lengthen and as the minutes passed, the browns and purples of the valleys grew noticeably deeper. Beyond the Arrochar hills and out towards the west the sky had become a haze of gold. No doubt the far side of Beinn Laoigh was afire with the sunset, but the eastern corrie, which faced me, was already grey and dead. I called to mind the dawn flush which had suffused those same snows so many hours before. Early in the afternoon a tracery of mackerel cloud had formed and built up to a tenuous grey canopy, but gradually this had been swept aside and now the wind itself had died away again. As the sun lost its power the cold grew steadily more intense. I shivered and creaked stiffly to my feet.

Half an hour later I was well down towards the burn below, the Allt Coire Ardrain, now cut off altogether from the sun by the shoulder of the Grey Height. Only a couple of miles of moorland separated me from the fleshpots of Crianlarich.

Whether or not all the Crianlarich tops have in fact been 'ridged' in a day, I have not been able to discover. It may well be that they have, for the expedition demands no more than an excess of energy and enthusiasm. Nor is the idea by any means new: seventy years ago it inspired an autumn attempt by a Scottish Mountaineering Club party of six, who travelled from Glasgow to Ardlui by the early morning West Highland train. It was not until 10.30 a.m. that they were across the Falloch at Beinn Ghlas farm and it is clear from their account that they were fighting a losing battle with the clock all day. They omitted Beinn Tulaichean and even then did not reach the cairn of Cruach Ardrain until an hour after sunset, so that there was no real hope of including Ben More and Stobinian. However, "the view of the tops of Cruachan standing out in inky outline against a narrow blood-red band in the western sky, which was all that remained of the sunset glow, formed one of the most glorious and impressive spectacles of the day". Descending in the dark alongside the Allt Coire Ardrain, "the jaded pedestrians stumbled into Crianlarich Station at nine o'clock", and were lucky enough to catch a late excursion train from Fort William back to Glasgow.

Perhaps one may be forgiven the indulgence of a satisfied chuckle.

4

The Outliers

Brine in the air, sunshine and wind on the face, and the heart
astir ... with great things awaiting you everywhere, everywhere.

C. E. Montague

EVER since that indefatigable explorer of the Western Isles,
Martin Martin, Gent., paid his remarkable visit to St. Kilda
in the summer of 1697, interest in the most remote island cluster
of the Hebrides has certainly never grown less. Today indeed,
almost three centuries later, it has reached far beyond all
reckoning.

Martin sailed out from Harris in an open boat, encountering
such a storm in the open Atlantic that his rowers were convinced their last days had come. They were out of sight of land
for sixteen hours and even when they reached the shelter of
Boreray, rather more than 4 miles from the main island of
Hirta, the weather continued so hostile that they were quite
surprised not to be driven hopelessly out to sea again.

Prior to the growth of tourism, communications between St.
Kilda and the outside world remained infrequent to say the
least. In the early nineteenth century one or two visits were
paid habitually each year by the factor—always provided the
weather was not too bad—but it was not until 1877 that John
McCallum's new cargo steamer *Dunara Castle*, with a full
complement of tourists, made the first of many successful
summer calls that were to last right down till 1939.

It was nearly a quarter of a century later, in September 1961,
that the first 'big ship' cruise taking in St. Kilda was organised
by the National Trust for Scotland; the second, also by M.S.
Dunera, took place early the following April, and I was fortunate
enough to be one of the hundreds of passengers who enjoyed a
particularly memorable trip. From the Firth of Forth and
circuits of the Bass Rock and the Isle of May, *Dunera* sailed
overnight up the East Coast for visits next day to those fascinating northern outliers Fair Isle and Foula. Our course was

then round Cape Wrath and down to the famous garden at Inverewe, followed by a crossing of the Minch to Stornoway. Here a welcome by the provost and an evening *ceilidh* to remember worked us up to keen anticipation of St. Kilda, the supreme climax of the cruise.

Some time after midnight *Dunera* moved out of Stornoway harbour, heading quietly up the Minch past Tiumpan Head and Tolsta Head, to turn west and south-west round the Butt of Lewis. From the Butt to St. Kilda was almost exactly 100 miles.

The run had been timed admirably in the cruise schedule: as we came out on deck after Sunday breakfast, stabbed abruptly by the north wind into keener wakefulness, there, faint as cloud-pencillings on the horizon, were the first stirring outlines of the whole St. Kilda group.

It was an ideal April morning. The long swell riding in from the North Atlantic had no venom in it and troubled us not at all. Early on, a fast-moving hail shower bore down on us out of a scud of black cloud, but thereafter the breeze swept the sky clear and left us to a day of superlative, unbroken sunshine. Mixed blues in abundance—amethyst and sapphire, turquoise and aquamarine—reached to our world's edge.

As the range closed to under 20 miles we were able to make out details: Boreray first and to the right, unmistakably, its dog-tooth outlier, Stac an Armin; beyond, the main islands of the group—Hirta and its serrated islet headland of Dun in the centre, with the highest ground on Soay just visible to its right and the splinter of rock, Levenish, on its own more than a mile off to the left. Sun-drenched, every line and tint was emerging vividly in the brisk morning air.

It was almost unbelievable that the weather should be favouring us in this way. The days before the start of the cruise had been wild with wind and rain and driving sleet—"Gales Lash Scots Shipping" the newspaper placards had proclaimed —so that as embarkation time approached, fireside comfort had seemed increasingly attractive. Even when the wind had swung round to the north and brought cold clear skies for the sail up the east coast, it had seemed too much to expect more than a very brief respite. St. Kilda, standing alone as it does so far out in the Atlantic, is a notorious cloud-maker and more often than not rain and mist lay siege to its high ground. "The hills," Martin commented, "are often covered with ambient white mists"; it is an observation which would probably be echoed by the great majority of visitors today.

I myself had seen the group once before, from some miles' distance one cold, mizzling evening during the war. From the deck of the troopship *Georgic*, bound for Iceland, I had looked across a desolation of restless waves to the gaunt grey cliffs rising like cathedral spires against a toneless grey sky. We on *Dunera* could hardly have complained if the whole scene had been similarly bleak and colourless and chill.

Yet up there on Boreray colour was outshining colour: ochre and tawny and rust, silver and white, vivid against the Alpine blue of the sky. The liner was brought close in under the cliffs, passengers crowding to the rails. We could see the wicked sea-polish of the rocks which, with their uncompromising steepness, makes them so nearly unassailable. The slopes above, turf and rock, climbed scarcely less steeply for more than 1,200 feet. Ridges reminiscent of the great buttresses of Ben Nevis, but more chaotically splintered into turrets and *aiguilles*, formed twin skyline edges that reached upwards and met like ruffled cocks' combs far, infinitely far, above. Black chimneys seamed the face, and shattered blocks, perched crazily, cluttered the sunlit crests. The spray which every now and again was flung high along the baseline was dwarfed to insignificance.

"This," wrote Dr. J. Morton Boyd, recalling one of his climbs to the summit crest of Boreray, "this was sea-cliff scenery *par excellence*—undoubtedly the finest that the British coasts afford and quite beyond description."

Some day possibly the rock-climbing experts will decide to try matching their prowess against the problems of these soaring sea-cliffs of Boreray. Attention has been turning more and more in recent years to the toughest challenges of the coast—to the Old Man of Hoy, to the Great Stack of Handa, not far south of Cape Wrath, to the fierce vertical slab of the Clett Rock springing provocatively from the breakers of the Pentland Firth—and inevitably the search keeps extending to newer, still more formidable defences to crack. St. Kilda will be an obvious choice and will have double attractions to offer—some of the most ferocious rocky-landings in the world and climbing

Gannets and Stac an Armin, St. Kilda

thereafter on knife-edge ridges which certainly look as though they lack nothing in exhilaration.

Quite slowly *Dunera* made down to Boreray's southern tip, to the final plunge of knife-edge and shadowed slabs. Then suddenly, almost unbelievably, the rock-curtain was past, disclosing with masterly stage-effect the fantastic wedge of Stac Lee, the 'coloured stack'.

Often enough in the past I have been overawed by sea-stacks —by the Old Man of Stoer, for instance, or the Stack of Handa—but here was one 200 feet higher than either of these, higher even than one of the spires of Cologne Cathedral. Stac Lee climbs sheer from blue-green depths to 544 feet, a grey, storm-sculptured monolith impressively alone, criss-crossed by diagonal ledges picked out in white by thousands of sitting gannets. "Stac Lee," wrote Dr. Julian Huxley, "must be the most majestic sea-rock in existence." It would, I decided, have been worth while coming on the cruise for that one glimpse alone.

In the old days Stac Lee used to be climbed every year as a matter of routine by the St. Kildan wildfowlers. At the end of the seventeenth century their harvest was said to amount to some 5,000 to 7,000 gannets—perhaps not too exaggerated a record, as Mr. James Fisher's count in 1939 put the total number of nests at 5,000, the birds on its bevelled top "crowded solidly at beak-range". The actual climb is apparently less difficult than it looks from a distance, the weathering of a basaltic dyke having gouged out a friendly ascending staircase for the greater part of the way. The first 150 feet are reputedly the hardest, lodgement on the rock having to be effected by throwing a rope over an iron peg on a hidden ledge. The whole ascent, however, according to the late Norman Heathcote who climbed the stack in July 1898 with his sister Evelyn and the famous St. Kildan Finlay McQueen, is not so difficult as the Inaccessible Pinnacle in Skye. Even so, the prospect of linking ledge and gutter high above the sea in an assault on that formidable face is one that is by no means comfortable to contemplate.

Passing clockwise outside Stac Lee, it was not many minutes before we were off its counterpart to the north-east, Stac an Armin, 'stack of the hero' or 'chief'. The latter is higher than

Village Bay, St. Kilda.
Dun in the background

Stac Lee by nearly 100 feet and used to have the reputation of being a more difficult climb. It is shaped more like a dog-tooth, one side falling in a vertical wall to the sea, the other tilted at a slightly less vicious angle. Here, too, the St. Kildans used to come after the sea-birds, and it has been said that 120 years ago one of their catches was a great auk, the last ever to be seen in Britain. According to the story, the men who captured it believed that it must be a witch and were so frightened that they beat it to death.

To the west of Borera [wrote Martin in 1698 after his remarkable voyage to St. Kilda] lies the rock Stack-Narmin, within pistol-shot; this rock is half a mile in circumference, and is as inaccessible as any of the above-mentioned; there is a possibility of landing only in two places, and that but in a perfect calm neither, and after landing the danger in climbing it is very great. The rock has not any earth or grass to cover it, and hath a fountain of good water issuing out above the middle of it, which runneth easterly: this rock abounds with solan geese and other fowls; here are several stone pyramids, as well for lodging the inhabitants that attend the seasons of the solan geese, as for those that preserve and dry them and other fowls, etc. The sea rises and rages extraordinarily upon this rock: we had the curiosity, being invited by a fair day, to visit it for pleasure, but it was very hazardous to us; the waves from under our boat rebounding from off the rock, and mounting over our heads wet us all, so that we durst not venture to land, though men with ropes were sent before us; and we thought it hazard great enough to be near this rock; the wind blew fresh, so that we had much difficulty to fetch St. Kilda again.

It was as we were passing Stac an Armin that we ran into the blizzard of gannets.

During the run in to the islands gannets had been everywhere; hundreds upon hundreds, weaving, speeding, crisscrossing, shearing the wave-tops. But here, off the stack, there must have been an immense shoal of fish immediately in the ship's wake, for the hundreds of birds were multiplied into thousands. They congregated in an incredible, milling, uncountable multitude, and as they plummeted into the water after the fish, they looked like shafts of white rain; there was no end to them, more and more thousands thronging from far and wide to join in the fun, swirling like snowflakes driven on the wind. How none collided, how never a wing-tip touched, is one of the mysteries of bird radar which is beyond understanding. It was clear from the excited commentaries coming over the ship's Tannoy that the ornithologists on board were highly delighted at witnessing this unique performance. Even for the layman it was now considerably easier to appreciate how the Boreray island group, with some 17,000 breeding pairs, is reckoned to be the largest gannetry in the world.

Having completed the circuit of Boreray and the Stacks, *Dunera* continued westwards towards the main island of Hirta. From the one group to the other is all of 4 miles, a distance that is not always appreciated, and it is not difficult to imagine the wickedly rough passages the St. Kildans must often have had to face here on their open-boat crossings. For us there was only pleasure: the wind sang, its touch keen as if straight from the Greenland ice-cap; the sun shone, blue sea mirroring blue sky.

Our course took us towards the edge of Conachair (1,397 feet), the highest point of St. Kilda and the highest sea-cliff in Britain. Here was fulmar rather than gannet territory, and soon we were enjoying the spectacle of a different kind of aerial mastery: quick wing-beats and effortless planing that took the birds in a never-ending confusion of comings and goings between surf-height and their chosen ledges high among the eaves of the cliff-face.

An estimate made not long after the last war put the St. Kilda population of fulmars at about 38,000 pairs, with half of these breeding on Hirta. The colony has, of course, been in existence at least since the seventeenth century and was of paramount importance to the island economy; indeed the very existence of the community depended on the gannet, the fulmar and the puffin. By 1758 the fulmar was replacing the gannet as favourite dish, while its feathers and oil were becoming more and more valuable commodities—in 1875 nearly 600 gallons of oil were exported from the island. Actual harvesting of the birds began every year on 12th August and lasted for from two to three weeks until, in 1903, the peak 'bag' of 12,000 birds was achieved and the inevitable decline set in.

It is another story altogether how St. Kilda was the only known fulmar breeding-station in Britain until 1878, when the island of Foula was colonised by birds from the Faeroes and Iceland, and how, so astonishingly far-reaching has been their spread, their nesting-places round the coasts of Scotland, England, Wales and Ireland now total several hundred.

From Conachair the high ground of Hirta, barren and wind-scoured, dips and climbs south-eastwards to Oiseval (948 feet), the eastern arm of Village Bay. As we cruised past Oiseval's lowest ramparts and came gradually into full sight of the heart of the island, I could not help reflecting with some satisfaction how this was a long-standing ambition that was being fulfilled. How many years was it, I wondered, since first I had thought of a trip to St. Kilda? Not that it had ever been anything more than a dream anyway, too improbable to be taken seriously; yet it had always been there at the back of my mind, one of those pleasantly vague notions like finding oneself in the Arctic or taking the road to Samarkand. Now here was reality: not, it is true, the complete satisfaction of a landing, but more than enough to be going on with.

By comparison it was amusing to think of the three or four dozen troops stationed on Hirta in connection with the Outer Hebrides guided weapons range. How many of these, I wondered, would be thinking of acknowledging their good fortune rather than railing at the ill luck that had taken them to this edge of nowhere, to Hirta, 'island of gloom'? It was possible to see something of their world through the glasses: the huddle of nissen huts on the flat ground in front of the ruins of the old houses and the road that snaked uphill, to the radar stations high above. Close inshore, towards the middle of the bay, a drifter rode at anchor.

The south-western arm of the Village Bay amphitheatre makes a graceful sweep round to Ruaival (444 feet) and thence to Dun, seemingly a headland but in reality a slender islet three-quarters of a mile long. Black sea-caves, deep surf-chiselled chimneys, shelves and ledges of gabbro, suggest endless possibilities for exploration—until, with a jerk, one is brought back to the realisation that these are among the most exposed rocks in the world, interminably pounded, remorselessly fretted and tunnelled by the unchecked fury of the Atlantic.

Large numbers of fulmars nest along the cliffs of Dun, with

shags and razorbills their neighbours. But above all it is the puffins, in countless, teeming, restless multitudes, which can really claim the island as their own. As we passed slowly round the outermost defences of fang and skerry, they scattered in their hundreds from the water and from the turf which capped the lichen-yellow rocks above. Just as the gannets of Boreray and the fulmars of Conachair had claimed our interest, so now we were diverted by a comedy of frantic splashings and fussings and whirrings. Before we quite realised it, we had rounded the islet's farthest tip and Village Bay was hidden once more from view.

The west coast of Hirta presents a particularly rugged and weather-beaten face to the Atlantic, rising from the surf-level caves and tunnels opposite Dun to a highest point of 1,164 feet on the crest of Mullach Bi. Tumbled rocks—looking from a distance like ordinary scree but often in reality as big as cottages —cover the less steep slopes, and here are the summer breeding-grounds of Manx shearwaters and of Leach's fork-tailed and storm petrels. Beyond Mullach Bi these western ramparts drop again more gradually to the Cambir (693 feet), then, with devastating finality, plunge to Soay Sound.

Here, as we passed, the sun vanished briefly behind a cloud and the wind struck more bleakly into our faces. The quarter-mile gap between Hirta and Soay seemed coldly inhospitable. Its three stacks—Stac Dona (47 feet), Stac Biorach (236 feet) and Soay Stac (200 feet)—were black fangs jutting wickedly from rings of surf on the surly grey of the sea. Imagination balked at picturing days of storm when all hell must be let loose in the wild insanity of the tide-jabble battling through the straits.

It was almost as difficult nevertheless to appreciate the contrasting picture painted by Dr. J. Morton Boyd:

> This is a truly wonderful place to be in a small boat on a calm summer's day. There is a fine choice of passages between mighty rocks through which to row. The boat emerges from the deep shadows of the stacks into the sparkling stream of sunlight, and the great towering fangs are continually changing their shapes. There are moments at St. Kilda when one becomes bemused by the magic of shadow and sunshine in savage places and by the intoxicating ocean air, but few places can excel Soay Sound for

sheer enchantment. The blue water is alive with seals and the sea-birds are there in their thousands. But one must fight against this bewitchment, for it is not a place to linger in too long.*

Almost literally from the cradle the St. Kildans of old acquired their unsurpassed skill in sea-cliff climbing. At the age of 3 the boys would start tackling the walls of the Village Bay cottages and it was not long before they were competing with each other on the actual cliffs in preparation for the hardest routes of all on the stacks. Every suitor for a local girl had to prove his affection, and also his expertness as a climber and breadwinner, by balancing on one foot and touching his toes, high up on the lintel of the celebrated 'mistress-stone'.

It was, however, on Stac Biorach in Soay Sound that the most exacting rock-route of all, the ultimate test of prowess was to be found. Apparently there was only one way up this stupendous sea *aiguille*, 50 feet higher than Nelson's Column, and that was fiercely difficult. Up it, towards the close of the last century, the alpinist R. M. Barrington was taken by the local 'tigers'.

> In about an hour's time [he wrote] we came to a narrow sound between the island of Soa and the large island, and the boat unexpectedly stopped before a perpendicular and in some places overhanging Stack, which looked to me absolutely inaccessible. The men talked in Gaelic, not a word of which I understood. One of them put a horse-hair rope around his waist. I could not imagine what they intended to do. For to ascend the rock immediately opposite appeared an utter impossibility, and my heart sank within me when they shouted "Stack-na-Biorrach, Stack-na-Biorrach!"
>
> Donald McDonald, the man with the horse-hair rope round his waist, stood in the bow of the boat. Another man held the rope slack, and, watching his opportunity as the boat rose on the top of a swell, McDonald jumped on a small ledge of slimy seaweed below high-water mark. There was a momentary stagger, but he kept his balance, and fastened himself to the rock by holding on apparently to the barnacles with which it was covered. He then proceeded upwards by sticking his fingers and toes into small wind-worn cavities on the western face. The rope was gradually slackened, and at a height of about thirty feet he turned

* *St. Kilda Summer*, by Kenneth Williamson and J. Morton Boyd (Hutchinson: 1960).

to the east, getting on a small narrow ledge, unseen from below which could not have been more than two or three inches wide. The whole of this performance was remarkable, especially having regard to its surroundings, the steeple-like rock rising from the ocean off the very wildest part of this remote island, the boatmen shouting in Gaelic to the climber, the great surge of the Atlantic threatening every minute to drive us against the cliff, and the horse-hair rope alternately slack and tightened as the boat rose and fell.

After a difficult lodgement and some hazardous climbing, Barrington found himself sharing a minute knob of rock with McDonald, 40 feet above the surf.

He pressed me against the face of the cliff, and, to my horror, Donald McQueen now proceeded to ascend the rope. For the life of me I did not know where he was going to stand, and to this day I am puzzled to know how we three men contrived to stand on this projection. Fearing every moment that I would fall, I shouted to pull the boat from the rock, so that in case of accident I should drop into the sea, and not into the boat from a distance of about forty feet. McQueen now put the rope round his waist and took the lead up a ledge two feet wide, wet with spray, which sloped at a very steep angle upwards. Having ascended this he grasped a narrow horizontal ledge about four inches wide and sloping outwards, so that the fingers slipped readily, and with his feet dangling in the air, proceeded to jerk himself along this ledge by getting a fresh hold every time with each hand alternately. It was about fifteen feet long. McDonald held the horse-hair rope which was round McQueen's waist, in his hand. This, no doubt, gave him a false sense of security but otherwise was absolutely useless, for, had McQueen fallen, they would have both tumbled into the sea.

It is with a feeling of profound relief that one reads of less exacting climbing still higher on the stack and of a successful end to the exploit.

The island of Soay, which lies beyond Soay Sound and its stacks, is less often mentioned than Hirta or the Boreray group. Perhaps because of this, one is apt to form the impression that it is rather tame, the poor relation as it were of the St. Kilda family. It is nothing of the sort. Immensely difficult of access— more awkward even than Boreray according to the descriptions—it is seldom visited nowadays and in recent times has had only the sketchiest exploration. Once a landing has been made, however, the climb to the highest point (1,225 feet) is said to be without difficulty and, with its remains of bothies and *cleitean*—the little stone cells in which the St. Kildans stored their crops and their harvests of sea-birds—was obviously well enough known to the islanders. Today the principal tenants of the storm-battered slopes are the shy Soay sheep.

As we rounded the island's western corner and passed slowly below its northern cliffs, we faced into bright sunlight. Skerries and rock-walls, caves and splintered aretes followed each other in succession, black and shadowed save where shafts of light slanted down as through cathedral windows. Momentarily I was reminded of the lonely coast of northern Iceland, an impression created in part by some unusual glimpses of snow, streaked and patchy on the summit crown of Cnoc Glas immeasurably high above. Then once again we were out in full sunlight, crossing the less formidable mouth of Glen Bay and approaching the familiar battlements of Conachair, to bring to an end our encirclement of the second group of islands.

Dunera had now completed a double loop; we could certainly have had no complaints if that had been the finish of the programme. But there was still a final variation to come. The Tannoy grated abruptly into life: "Attention, please. We are now going to return to Boreray. The Commander has decided to 'thread the needle'—to take *Dunera* through the gap between Boreray and Stac Lee. We can promise you, I know, one of the real highlights of the cruise."

Ten minutes brought us back once again to Boreray. Slowing to manoeuvre into position, the ship's bows slewed round on target with the ponderous precision of a siege-gun. Up for'ard the deck swarmed even more busily than before, every inch of the rails crowded in expectation.

Very slowly, very majestically, *Dunera* closed the gap. On the one hand the cock's comb of Boreray, almost hanging over us now, climbed in slab and slat and knife-edge to its unseen summit crest. On the other, vividly coloured in the sunshine, the great sea-stack crowded upon us even more closely; soon we were craning our necks to glimpse far above the highest of its ledges and the white multitudes of the gannets.

Steadily the gap narrowed, Boreray's brown wall only yards

away to starboard. Momentarily the shadow of the stack fell across the deck as we idled past. Then, almost suddenly it seemed, we were through, swaying and swinging widdershins round the sunless north face. The last, most impressive circuit was complete.

It was a few minutes before midday. There was just time if one hurried to reach the assembly hall for Sunday morning service. I joined the queue and went in. The opening hymn, "Now thank we all our God", seemed more than ordinarily appropriate.

Later I came out on deck once again. We were heading south. South into the sun. For long I stood looking back, watching the great cliffs shrink in size and their details gradually fade. The miles lengthened and imperceptibly Hirta and Boreray merged into one. For a little longer they hung like a faint grey cloud, slowly dissolving. Then, almost surprisingly, the horizon was empty.

It was another eight years before the opportunity occurred to see St. Kilda again and I was able at last to realise my ambition to set foot ashore at Village Bay.

Thanks to the generosity of the army authorities, permission was given me early in 1970 to make a round trip in one of the Royal Corps of Transport supply ships. By choosing a date not too far on in the summer it was confidently hoped that the seas would be calm and the sunshine suitably idyllic—a hope which the Atlantic duly made quite sure was not fulfilled.

The trip began at 2200 hours precisely on a blustery Monday evening of mid-May, when H.M. Army Vessel *Abbeville*, alias Landing Craft Tank No. 4041, left Helensburgh pier bound for South Ford, Benbecula, in the Outer Isles, and after that Village Bay, St. Kilda.

The run that was just beginning was to be typical—so far as any such journeys ever can be described as typical—of the vital service that has to be maintained, in fair weather and in foul, re-supplying the most isolated army stations in Britain. Already in the comfortable little wardroom, with its crest-decorated walls and its soothing stereophonic tape-music, my companion George Alden and I had met Captain John Bull and his first and second officers, Peter May and Bryon Harness;

now, from the bridge, as the Cloch lighthouse and the serried
street-lights of Gourock began to slip astern into the gathering
darkness, we peered down into the black belly of the tank deck
and saw the purpose of it all—the cargo that only such landing-
craft can ship to the islands: heavily laden trailers which,
once the doors go down on the beaches, can be towed ashore by
Scammells; a Land-Rover; a compressor; two massive, ungainly
caravans.

We took to our bunks somewhere beyond Toward Point,
the breeze obviously freshening. In fact a gale warning was
out—first of a pattern that was to become almost laughably
monotonous—and off the Mull of Kintyre in the early hours of
the following morning the *Abbeville* was rolling to a long, unfriendly swell. "Not to worry," Number One had assured us,
tongue in cheek, "we can ship 500 tons of water before we sink.
As a matter of fact, even if we were in two halves we should be
able to keep floating all right." I turned over and dozed off
again; it seemed pointless to wonder which half of the ship to
choose.

It is only during the summer period, approximately from the
beginning of April until the end of September, that the Army
L.C.T.s maintain this supply service from Rhu, near Helensburgh, to Benbecula and St. Kilda. Two of the eleven belonging to the Royal Corps of Transport were being used at that
time, with a third due to join in for the final weeks in September.
The total schedule for the season comprised fifteen sailings with
occasional 'as required' runs in between whiles.

On St. Kilda the military garrison of just over thirty is res-
ponsible for the constant manning of surveillance radars in
order to ensure the air and sea safety of the Hebridean rocket
range. At present much of the firing from South Uist is
meteorological, for the Science Research Council, but, as during
military rocket firing, the range has to be kept clear. In 1970,
too, Village Bay was a particularly busy place, as new radar
was being installed, a re-housing programme was going on and
a more serviceable jetty was being built: all strangely alien to
the peace and quiet of Hirta.

During the winter months the St. Kilda service is kept going
—although for personnel and light stores only—by the Isles
class trawler *Mull*, another R.C.T. vessel, but civilian manned.

At Village Bay the final ferrying ashore is carried out by a small open dory, the *Puffin*, more often than not in savage weather and darkness.

It is, I decided on our first morning out, a rare pleasure while shaving to be able to look out of a porthole and watch Manx shearwaters dipping their wings to the wave-crests; satisfying, too, to be able in half a gale to meet the mess-steward's eye when he asks: "What would you like for breakfast, sir—bacon, eggs, tomatoes, fried bread, baked beans?" His query was in fact an earnest of the excellent feeding in the days ahead, from roast chicken or steak, kidney and mushroom pie to a curry of oriental exquisiteness.

Breakfast over, we savoured that first morning to the full: showers storming at us over the Mull of Oa; sunshine and a cutting wind in the Sound of Islay; fine views in impressive sequence of the west coast of Jura. Then, as there was time to spare to suit the tides, we put in to Oban for an afternoon's shopping.

Meanwhile the *Abbeville* was acquiring the cheerful, even hilarious familiarity of home. Captain Bull—a Somerset man and formerly a sapper until his transfer to the newly formed R.C.T. in 1965—played host to memorable perfection. Nothing, it was reassuringly obvious, could repress his sense of fun. Under his genial eye no moment could ever reasonably be dull—a fact which was noticeably reflected in the happy spirit throughout the ship.

During the afternoon the weather had worsened and as we swung out of Oban Bay it was bleak, misty and cold. A coaster lying stranded and abandoned on Lady Rock off Lismore, just distinguishable in the thickening dusk, hardly seemed the best of auguries; nor were we greatly comforted by gale forecasts for every area from South-East Iceland to the North Sea. The wild tide-jabble off Ardnamurchan Point came all too soon after the sanctuary of the Sound of Mull.

Most of the following day, Wednesday, was spent at South Ford, Benbecula. Here the entrance channel, threading through wicked reefs port and starboard, is intricate in the extreme. At its narrowest it is between 70 and 80 feet wide—not so very much more than the 39 foot 4 inch beam of L.C.T. 4041. A tearing wind does little to help. Approach must be made at high tide and it is then necessary to wait for the great flat expanse of sand to dry out. Thereafter, of course, sailing-time must wait once again for the flood. For us there was constant interest in all the trials and tribulations of off-loading through the gaping tunnel-mouth of the tank deck; then, operations completed, the army vehicles made off across the sand like scurrying black beetles. The doors were closed and secured. Slowly the tide seeped in again, covering sand and seaweed and skerries. And all the while the ship's aerials and rigging, flailed by the wind, whined with a growing shrillness that boded ill for the coming night.

From South Ford our course lay 20 miles up the sheltered east side of Benbecula and North Uist, then out westwards again through another channel of ill repute, the Sound of Harris. We reached there well on in the evening, the low sun throwing an unreal dazzle over the flanking reefs and tide-rips. Here and there gannets were cruising over the spindrift, although ominously, above one of the islets, a party of shags could make no headway at all in take-off against the sheer malice of the gale.

Then almost suddenly we were through and off the shoulder of Pabbay, facing the full weight of the Atlantic swell. At once the bow was lifting over grey-white mountains, dropping as rapidly beyond. Waves and troughs were gigantic, one at least well above bridge-height. It was the sort of heaving malevolent maelstrom which it is only bearable to look at by keeping one's eyes tightly closed. There was no consolation in the reflection that this kind of thing just shouldn't be happening in the month of May; it quite simply was. For a while we fought into it, bows tossing like a fairground 'waltzer'. But though persever-ance might have been possible, it would certainly not have been pleasant. We swung away north, therefore, up the coast of Harris, to seek shelter behind the island of Taransay at the mouth of West Loch Tarbert. Even the passengers felt almost worthy of the rum ration that was issued once the anchor was down. That night, we heard, there were seven trawlers shelter-ing in Village Bay, St. Kilda.

The following day gave better promise. We lost track of time as the wind began to drop and brilliant sunshine gradually won the upper hand. Some of us even managed a brief visit of exploration to Taransay, bouncing in the ship's boat through defences of explosive surf. But we were impatient now for journey's end, and with wind and sea obviously relenting at last, the captain's assurance that we would be under way again during the night was more than welcome.

It was 0745 hours when I came on deck next morning, and there—9 miles distant, according to the radar screen—was the familiar outline. Sunless this time and grey; aloof beyond the slow Atlantic swell, but, as always, profoundly stirring. Boreray and the Stacks; farther off, Levenish, Dun and the softer outlines of Hirta itself. And in between, as if to welcome us back, innumerable gannets and fulmars.

Slowly, almost irksomely slowly we swayed the last miles, while the great cliff of Conachair grew and grew in immensity, busy everywhere with fulmars. Then the scene changed again: the huge wall was lost once more to sight as we turned in under the slatted brown eaves of Oiseval. We were in Village Bay at last. A few minutes' circling while we waited for the tide, then, with the sand just beginning to show yellow, we ran in for touchdown.

Unfortunately, in the immediate prospect ashore there was little enough to please: stacks of oil drums, stark concrete buildings, scars of road-works; over the half-built new jetty a crane hanging like a threat; bulldozers and dumptrucks, Land-Rovers and tractors, all seemingly in a frenzy of activity; somewhere a compressor clattering away like a machine-gun. Only one thing cheered me: now and again above the bedlam I could hear the St. Kilda wrens bursting into irrepressible song.

No doubt, of course, this is all a part of the new history of St. Kilda, history which began in April 1957 with Operation 'Hardrock' and occupation by the R.A.F. working from Cairn Ryan, down in Wigtownshire. Later the Royal Artillery took over and Rhu became the mainland base when Cairn Ryan was closed. Some day the story will be told in full and an interesting one it will be too, with impressions perhaps by some of those most closely concerned—the signallers or the cooks who do six-week stretches three or four times a year, the commanding officers who measure their spells in from six to nine months, some of the contractor's men who have certainly earned the right to wear the coveted 'Puffin' tie for residence on the island.

On the average, it is said, the men like Kilda—the 'St.' is customarily discarded—even those for whom duty there is the most improbable of contrasts. Surprisingly perhaps so far as transport to and from the island is concerned, it is only in life and death emergencies that use is made of helicopters, so treacherous are the wind-currents over Village Bay. There is, however, an entitlement to one air-drop a week for mails and urgent supplies, and for this Cessna aircraft are used, coming in low through the gap between Oiseval and Conachair.

For our own landing we were borne aloft triumphantly in a mechanical digger to allow us to remain dryshod. Thereafter there was much to do—and sadly little time in which to do it. I had had a grandiose plan to visit the summit of Conachair, then drop down to Glen Bay on the far side of Hirta, to the ramp and tunnel at Gob na h'Airde, that scenic showpiece of cliffs and sea-surge where in summer the grey seals lie and bask. On the way back up Gleann Mor to the watershed there would have been the celebrated Amazon's House and the ancient neighbouring dwellings to examine. But a programme as ambitious as this was unfortunately out of the question; instead I did what so may other visitors have had to do in short spells ashore—I wandered down beside the crumbling cottages of Main Street, "the saddest street in all Scotland"; took interested looks at the innumerable stone *cleitean*, the primitive St. Kildan storehouses, and tried optimistically to photograph the chocolate-brown Soay sheep and their lambs.

This, however, was scarcely satisfying. Having made certain that I had at least one good view of a St. Kilda wren—singing its head off on a heap of salty-grey stones—I turned off into the great moorland bowl behind the village. Here, on the short, wind-scoured turf, I was chided by an agitated pair of oyster-catchers, while snipe flew drumming overhead in sweeps so fast that they looked hopelessly out of control. In a few hundred yards I had left the chill new world of concrete behind and stepped into the true friendliness of the islands.

Inevitably the moor led upwards, gently at first then more steeply, to the Gap, the lowest point of the ridge which links the dome of Oiseval with the higher slopes of Conachair.

Abruptly one comes to a sandy edge, and there just beyond is a breath-taking drop of 550 feet to skerries and creaming surf. Over 4 miles away, grey outlines on grey sea, are Boreray and the Stacks. Only the fulmars and the guillemots whirring far below about the black fang of Stac a' Langa give comprehensible clues to the scale.

Oiseval itself (948 feet) was not far below the mist-fringe now trailing over the highest ground of Conachair. It still gave fine views, however, of the whole sweep of Village Bay, with the *Abbeville* central to the arc of beach curling round to the out-thrust battlements of Dun. I was struck particularly by the extensive scattering of the *cleitean*, which were dotted far and wide up the hill-slopes and not merely round the outskirts of the village. Some of the islanders must have had plenty of walking to do to reach their stores of peat-turves and hay and everything pertaining to their harvest of sea-birds from the cliffs.

The weather unfortunately was deteriorating, and while I was at lunch aboard the *Abbeville* the mist crept down almost to sea-level. There was not much obvious inducement to go ashore again; only the realisation that time on Hirta is always precious and that I might never be there again sent me obediently down the tank deck ramp to the sand and the rough boulder-field beyond.

In the event I had an afternoon walk that was wet, clammy, almost wholly without views—and immensely enjoyable. Sheep-tracks led across the westward scree-slopes towards Ruaival and the narrow passage between Hirta and Dun, and these I followed for perhaps half a mile. Below, where rock-walls and sea met, I could see occasional parties of eiders, and on the grey-green cliffs farther round I took the dotted pattern of white to be a small colony of kittiwakes. Instead of the same way back, a shallow gully led upwards into blank mist for several hundreds of feet. Visibility was perhaps 20 yards, but imagination knew no bounds at all and it was possible to picture a day of sunshine and an immensity of blue ocean and blue sky, with a foreground beneath the feet of the first line of cliff defences, alive with interminably restless seabirds.

The tide was flooding once more as I crossed the few yards of sand and regained the dark maw of the *Abbeville*'s tank deck.

By 1700 hours we were away. All around at the mouth of the bay countless puffins and guillemots were swimming and against the jagged background of Dun the traffic was incessant; once a great skua hurried past, no doubt on piracy bent. The man-made noise and bustle ashore were already forgotten; there was the real St. Kilda, the St. Kilda which can never disappoint.

Our run home was faster by approximately a day and a half. Not that it was direct, as can sometimes be the way; we had to call once again at South Ford and submit there to the un-hurried dictatorship of the tides. But the weather was more benevolent now and the only seeming hazard was some thick sea-mist which brought the radar into play as we threaded through the Sound of Harris. We passed Skerryvore during Saturday night, rounded the Mull of Kintyre in an unexpected return of sunshine and survived the throng of week-end yachtsmen to touch down uneventfully at Rhu the following evening. It was exactly forty-eight hours since we had left Village Bay; almost six days since our original departure from Helensburgh.

As we said our goodbyes, it was clear that thoughts aboard the *Abbeville* were already busy with the immediate future—a quick turn round and return once more to St. Kilda. No doubt just another routine run.

Approach to the hills.
In Gleann na Muice

5

The Hills

It is rather a problem deciding what you must take and what you can leave behind, but it is amazingly simplified when you know that you have to carry it all yourself.

H. W. Tilman

Up in Wester Ross, to the north of Loch Maree and behind the mighty mountain-barrier of Slioch, lies some of the wildest country in Britain. It is an area of quiet lochans and clamorous burns, of pitilessly rough moorland and proud, desolate hills. Yet so great are the distances, so formidable the difficulties of access, that visitors are unusually rare. During the stalking season it is, like many other fine corners of the Highlands, a forbidden area. In winter the door is closed with almost the same finality by the short span of daylight. Indeed it is only in spring and early summer that there are good opportunities of turning plans for exploration into truly satisfying realities.

Theo Nicholson and I had for long been impatient to head north on a visit. The area was almost entirely new to both of us and the invitation of its hills was too pressing to be ignored indefinitely. Our first planning had been for spring, but in the end it was late in May before we were able to escape from our respective desks, bound for Kinlochewe.

The weather could not really have been described as seasonable. About the middle of the preceding week the temperature had begun to drop and by the time Friday came round there was more than a touch of Arctic cold in the air. The afternoon, as we drove up Loch Lomondside, was bitter, and farther north, as we rounded Loch Leven, the gulls were swinging into an icy wind over waters of battleship grey. Dusk came about us, cheerless and bleak, as we hurried through Drumnadrochit and Beauly and Garve, and by the time we had passed Achnasheen and were dropping down to Kinlochewe Hotel through that ultimate of desolation, Glen Docherty, we felt as if we had stepped back into January. Evening merged into a

The ruined bothy and Sgurr an Tuill Bhain

night of sheeting rain and when we peered out of the hotel windows next morning, there was fresh snow on the hills down to 1,500 feet.

Our original plan of campaign had been conceived on the grand scale: we would, we decided, follow the 30-mile mountain switchback that stretches without too many breaks from Kinlochewe to Dundonnell—a kind of high-level route over Slioch, the central barrier of hills beyond Lochan Fada and that monarch of a dozen tops, An Teallach. With the addition of one or two rock-climbing refinements *en route*, such a journey would surely be one of the finest mountain exploits in Scotland.

Unfortunately this was much too ambitious. The time we had available was not sufficient and the transport arrangements which would have been necessary were too elaborate to be made at short notice. Instead of the complete traverse to Dundonnell, we decided to concentrate on the middle section only, on that magnificent quartet of hills with the names that look like extracts from the Gaelic dictionary: A'Mhaighdean, Beinn Tarsuinn, Mullach Coire Mhic Fhearchair and Sgurr Ban. Two of these, we reckoned, would be of especial interest— A'Mhaighdean, 'the maiden', which enjoyed the description of "one of the most remote hills in Scotland", and Beinn Tarsuinn, 'the crosswise mountain', which had achieved distinction as the missing 'Munro'.

It is amusing to recall that barely eighty years ago the most authoritative list of the Scottish mountains was that of Baddeley's Guide. This gave a mere thirty-one summits of over 3,000 feet in height. It was only in 1891 that the picture was completely altered by the publication of Sir Hugh Munro's Tables; in the latter the total of 3,000-foot mountains had been multiplied nearly ten times.

Munro's Tables have, of course, been amended and revised in various ways since they were first published, but it was not until 1929 that a claim was put forward for the inclusion of Beinn Tarsuinn. The true height of this hill, 3,080 feet, had been missed by the Ordnance Survey and it was argued by mountaineers that it deserved a better fate than to be left on the maps as a mere contour line below the 3,000-foot level. In the end it was admitted to the 1953 Edition but, amusingly enough, it was such a latecomer that it could not be given a place in the order of precedence, nor could the official total of 276 separate Scottish mountains be altered.

With the four Gaelic 'Munros' as our main objectives, Theo and I set off from Kinlochewe in a feeble gleam of after-breakfast sunlight. Armed with permission from Mr. Roddy Campbell, the head keeper, we took the road to the Heights of Kinlochewe. This is quite motorable in an honest, rugged way, and for 3 miles keeps close to the bank of the Abhainn Bruachaig. We passed a couple with a caravan and commented approvingly on the site they had chosen, beside a waterfall and cauldron pool, with superb views back to the sharp ridges of Beinn Eighe.

A few scattered cottages comprise the Heights of Kinlochewe, but we saw no one about as we parked the car and started to make up our loads of equipment and food. It was soon apparent that these were going to be staggering. One particularly bulky item to be carried was my tent. I had previously had my doubts about this, as one afternoon when it had been pitched in the garden, its walls had provided some entertaining climbing for our cat. As a result its waterproof qualities seemed to have been rather seriously impaired and I decided to try and borrow a substitute from a friend. The latter is a Himalayan traveller of no little renown and the possibility of failure never entered my head. But my mission did in fact prove fruitless after all. Truly misfortune is no respecter of persons. His tent had been eaten by a horse.

The aptitude for travelling light is something that has always, unfailingly, passed me by. Perhaps it is because, as Stewart Edward White put it: "You can no more be told how to go light than you can be told how to hit a ball with a bat. It is something that must be lived through." However that may be, I found myself on this occasion bent to a hairpin stoop. The fact that Theo was carrying as much as I was, if not a good deal more, was not the slightest consolation. All it seemed to prove to me was that, at our time of life, we ought to have known a great deal better.

The sun meanwhile had become much stronger and although a blustery wind obviously had more heavy showers in store, the snow-line had retreated far uphill. Our approach march was evidently going to be warm.

So, indeed, it proved. The track we followed was a good one—negotiable by jeep for about a mile and a half—but it was a steady upwards grind and our burdens were mountainous. Nor was the scenery particularly attractive, the whole of this part of Gleann na Muice being shut in and devoid of distant views. We stopped to cool off beside the burn, where a wooden bridge spans a miniature gorge, thankfully lowering our bloated rucksacks to the bank. Then, with our second wind, we made better time up the rest of the climb.

For a further mile and a half the ground levelled off, a sandy footpath threading its way through humps and hillocks of young heather. Here, with quite surprising abruptness, the panorama of our hills opened out. It was what we had been waiting and toiling for, and we looked eagerly at the exhilarating sweep of the skyline. Far to the left, snow-brindled slopes climbed gently to the summit of A'Mhaighdean; in the centre Beinn Tarsuinn, broad and bulky, caught the flooding tide of sunlight; right, the brown moor ended suddenly below the pinnacled south-eastern ridge of Mullach Coire Mhic Fhearchair. Over all arched wind-tormented sky of grey and blue. It was a view which, with its spaciousness, its immense breadth and depth, seemed to epitomise in a moment this whole magnificent bit of country. We were certainly not disappointed.

During our previous planning we had heard a rather vague rumour that there was a bothy hereabouts, and a minute black pinpoint on the map seemed to bear this out. We therefore kept a good look out with high hopes of finding a really luxurious base camp. It came into sight round a bend in the path—a bothy in a delightful situation overlooking Lochan Gleann na Muice. Unfortunately, however, our optimism died a swift death. Close inspection of the bothy showed it to be little better than a shell, with at least half the roof gone and the whole south-east corner supported by a keystone no bigger than a cricket ball. The floor was littered with a jumble of masonry and this in turn was surmounted by beams and rafters in equally wild confusion. Altogether the whole place gave the impression of having been in ruins for a long time, and I was amused to have this view borne out later on, after our return home, when I came across a reference by a climber of thirty years ago. His comment read: "The only vestige of civilisation passed on the way was a bothy that had evidently been quite recently struck by lightning, for its northern gable was scattered about the hillside."

With the weather as doubtful as it was, we thought at first of avoiding the hazards of the tent by taking up residence inside the bothy itself. However, the draughts which assailed us from almost every direction at once, and the precarious equilibrium of the masonry which was still standing, prompted us to think again. Finally we decided to compromise. We set up kitchen and dining-room indoors among the debris and established our sleeping quarters in the tent, which we pitched on a mossy strip not far from the front door. The patches that I had slapped so merrily on the fabric, over the cat's claw-marks, would have to be put to the test after all.

Meanwhile the rain was holding off, and as we busied ourselves with lunch, the sun flooded across the moors and spun an attractive pattern of light and shade on Sgurr an Tuill Bhain, eastern bastion of Slioch. Ridges of grass and rock, tapered to a graceful spire, seemed to have been expressly designed to put an end to any thoughts of an afternoon siesta. As soon, therefore, as we had finished eating, we packed light rucksacks—featherweights by comparison with those of the morning—and took blithely to the ups and downs of the heather.

My chief recollections of the subsequent exercise are of our two river-crossings. It was after a mile and a half of the moor that we were brought up short by the Abhainn an Fhasaigh, at first glance just a broad burn flowing doucely out of Lochan Fada. Optimistically we looked for a bridge; then, a little less certainly, we looked for stepping-stones; finally we looked for an easy ford. But all we discovered was the depth of the channel and the violence of the current—particularly where it gathered speed to whip round a bend and disappear like the Royal Scot into the tunnel-canyon of Gleann Bianasdail. I sat down resignedly on the bank, removed my boots and stockings and took the first shuddering steps into snow-chilled depths.

We had, of course, to repeat the crossing on the way back, a pleasure to which we looked forward with remarkably little enthusiasm. In between, however, we roamed enjoyably up the slender ridge of Sgurr an Tuill Bhain, and Theo, more energetic than I, continued the additional mile to Slioch's main top. Slioch (3,217 feet) is a particularly fine mountain, photographed times without number in views from the main road on the far side of Loch Maree. I had been up it once a number of years previously and remembered it especially well from an incident which occurred at the summit. It was a day of thick, eddying mist, and as we sat eating our lunch, a golden eagle suddenly appeared, obviously intending to alight on the cairn beside us. Immediately he saw us, of course, he swung away again into the sanctuary of the mist, but not before we had had a rare impression of the bold markings and immense wing-span.

On our climb Theo and I were struck once again by the spaciousness of this lonely, rugged country, with a constantly changing outlook over Lochan Fada and the great flat plateau above Gleann Bianasdail, wild as the Rough Bounds of Knoydart or the lava areas of Iceland. Even though the mist clapped a grey blanket about us above 2,500 feet, the whole outing rewarded us richly and gave us a shrewd foretaste of what was in store for us on the morrow.

Back at the bothy we settled down to the serious business of supper. The Abhainn an Fhasaigh and the tribulations of the moor had given us appetites that clamoured for the highest flights of culinary skill. Theo had brought his usual contribution of pemmican, so that this inevitably became the main course on the menu. In my day I have worked my way through not a few of Theo's efforts—some good, some bad and some frankly indifferent. This one promised to fall into a fourth category, beyond the power of words to describe. Quite early on he had remarked: "I'm putting in everything except the soap." Later, however, I could not escape the conclusion that he must have had second thoughts and gone the whole hog.

During the night it rained. Sharp, heavy blatters that drummed and rattled on the tent fabric, jerking us every now and again into sudden wakefulness. Luckily the ravages of the cat had been satisfactorily countered and we were not troubled by a single leak.

Theo brought me my morning cup of tea—no doubt hoping to shame me into activity—and in due course I condescended to take a look outside. It was the sort of morning to send one back to one's sleeping-bag: heavy grey clouds rolling up from the south on a warm, moist wind. A curtain of rain was drifting lazily towards us across the heather. Prospects could scarcely have looked less attractive.

We had been thinking all along in terms of visiting the eastern hills of the group first and working westwards. Now, however, the weather prompted us to change this plan. It would be more sensible, we decided, to make first for A'Mhaighdean, the farthest away of the 'Munros'. For one thing the long approach might as well be done in the rain and there was always the chance that conditions might improve later on. For another, if the worst came to the worst and we could 'bag' only one of the peaks, the most inaccessible was the obvious choice; we might even be able to make a quick dash for the nearer tops the following morning.

We decked ourselves out, therefore, to look like cox'n and mate of the Kinlochewe lifeboat and set out on the switchback path leading north-west to Lochan Fada. We faced the prospect of at least 4 unusually arduous miles before we even started to climb A'Mhaighdean. This was not at all attractive, for we knew that once the track ended at the lochside the going would be atrocious. It proved to be worse, much worse. Indeed, I think the moorland was the roughest I have ever encountered. If I had been a horse, I am sure it would have reminded me of the Grand National. The heather was deep and as tough as fence-wire. Some of the banks seemed steeper than breaking waves, while down in the hollows between, boulders lay concealed for no other purpose than to fray the temper. Perhaps if the morning had been fresher, we might have felt happier, but it was warm and muggy, so that we had to keep choosing between feeling too hot with waterproof clothing on or becoming extremely wet without it—always a particularly difficult choice to make.

Some idea of the terrain may perhaps be gathered from the experience of a friend of mine who was passing one day close to Lochan Fada on his way back from a climb. As he was toiling over a particularly rough stretch, he happened to catch sight of a hind some distance ahead, accompanied by a calf no more than a day or two old. Hoping for a photograph, he worked his way forward to close range through the jungle of heather, noting the while that the hind had moved away on her own up the hillside. He knew exactly where the calf had been left; he was quite certain, within a radius of a few yards, where it must be lying hidden, and he was determined to get the photograph. But, try as he would over every foot of the ground, he never found that fawn.

For us, fortunately, there were compensations for the rough going. The wind and rain were at our backs and consequently much less troublesome than they might have been. We could watch the grey clouds spilling incessantly over the great hog's back of Slioch and fanning out across Lochan Fada, while Slioch itself was always impressive, its western ramparts a black threat to assault. Still farther on we were tremendously impressed by our views of the Beinn Lair cliffs—buttress after buttress plunging from summit plateau to glen floor in majestic succession as far as the eye could reach. This wonderful mountain face is of unusual interest to the rock-climber, for it is one of the most remarkable 'discoveries' of recent years. Apart from a single reconnaissance carried out in May 1909 by those almost legendary pioneers of the North-west, W. N. Ling and G. T. Glover, the crags remained virtually unknown until the summer of 1951. Then, by strange coincidence, no less than five climbing parties paid visits of exploration within a space of three months. Some of the routes they opened up on the steep gneiss buttresses were as much as 800 feet in length and worthy to be rated among the best climbs of the Northern Highlands.

We stopped for an early lunch—or maybe it was second breakfast—in the lee of a rock-spire like Cleopatra's Needle. It was good to rest for a little from our antics on the moor and to be able to sit back in comfort while a fresh squall of rain stormed harmlessly past. We felt that all our foot-slogging had really earned us the right to embark on A'Mhaighdean and we looked eagerly at the steepening slopes ahead.

Our brief snack over, we slanted up between some rocky bluffs, thankfully leaving the deep heather behind. Soon we found ourselves on a slope that climbed at a uniform angle into a distant drift of mist. We plodded upwards rhythmically and with little talk. At times we zigzagged far apart, at others we almost trod on one another's heels on the short turf, while

whenever we veered farther left than usual, we discovered even
more striking views of Beinn Lair; the great grey wall of cliffs
seemed to emphasise the more our own rather placid highway.
Higher still, a covey of ptarmigan broke away from a patch of
scree with a whirr of wings and rude, guttural scolding. And
all the while we kept up our mechanical plod, plod, towards the
grey mist-cap. At last we reached it and, more thankfully still,
the crown of summit rocks overtopped by the cairn. The long
gentle slope we had ascended had firmly convinced us that The
Maiden was a very tame mountain indeed.

Then, quite suddenly, we knew we were wrong. The breeze
freshened and, eddying round the rocks, tore open a window
in the clouds. We stood amazed at what we saw. At our feet the
ground fell sheer into nothingness. We looked straight down on
to the silver sickle of the Dubh Loch 2,500 feet below and,
beyond a thin dividing causeway, Fionn Loch leading away
north-west to the desolation of moors behind Aultbea and
Poolewe. It was a picture of a few brief seconds, then the curtain
of the mist fell back and visibility shrank once more to a few
woolly feet. Eagerly we waited for more. In an excess of optimism we even fished out our cameras. But although the window
half opened again several times, we added little to our know-
ledge except vague glimpses of the fine steep north-west ridge.
We had had our quota of luck. Soon the mist came swirling
more thickly about us, damp and clammy on our faces.

But we had seen quite enough to appreciate how utterly
mistaken we had been in dismissing The Maiden as dull. It
was obvious to us now that it was a mountain of rugged
character, full of tremendous climbing possibilities if approached
from that formidable western flank. We thought gratefully of
those few moments during which its secrets had been so boldly
revealed.

The breeze which had flung open the windows in the mist had
freshened still more for our return downhill. Gradually it
began to cause confusion among the marching cloud-rack. It
even allowed the sun to burst through and we luxuriated in the
feel of genuine warmth, so different from the hothouse steami-
ness of the upward trail. Here and there wet slabs of rock
started to glint and shimmer like polished shields, and even the
ground underfoot seemed more brightly coloured with the

promise of summer heat. Away through to the north, beyond a giant's notch of converging hill-slopes, we glimpsed the spires and turrets of An Teallach.

The bealach between A'Mhaighdean and Beinn Tarsuinn, our next objective, had rather a familiar look about it—bog and heather and pool and rock in the same mixture as before. It was almost half a mile wide and, at under 1,700 feet, the lowest saddle of the day. But at least it had one thing to commend it—a mossy sun-trap where we allowed ourselves the luxury of fifteen lazy minutes—fifteen minutes in which to savour, like a king's sherry, the pleasure of honest work accomplished and easy scorn for the stiffer brae ahead.

To lie back and feel the full, free warmth of the sun, tempered by no more than a light touch of breeze, is surely one of the supreme joys of a day on the hills. It can really be earned only by hard toil, it can be captured only on the right day, but always it is worth working and waiting for. So on this occasion, as we gazed idly up at the drifting clouds or down to Larachantivore and the green oasis of Strath na Sheallag, we were satisfied. A mere quarter of an hour had in it more than enough inspiration to lighten the tedium of another 1,400 feet.

But Beinn Tarsuinn is in any case a fine mountain in its own right, with no monotony in its make-up. We soon discovered that more than mere height gives it a character worthy of 'Munro' status. Above the first steep rise, gay in its sunlit purples and browns, we reached a narrow arête. Here the grey rock tapered to a knife-blade, notched and stepped in pleasant sequence. Blocks, splintered and chaotic, climbed to the crest on the side of our approach, while beyond, the rim of a corrie fell away even more sharply. A succession of pinnacles suggested the delights of Stack Polly or of the Aonach Eagach, above Glencoe.

"What a grand bit of ridge!" I heard Theo muttering, as he edged along the sill of a tall square-cut pillar which we had already noticed from a long way away, set boldly against the skyline. "Just a pity we haven't time to explore here more fully."

I would have agreed with him wholeheartedly, but conversation had suddenly become difficult. On the sheltered lower slopes we had forgotten about the wind, but now it struck at us harshly, whisking our words into space and doing its best to throw us off balance. There was a bite in it too, for an army of clouds had again been on the march, massing against the sun. The quick change took us by surprise and set us fairly racing over the eaves and corners of the ridge in a concerted effort to keep warm. We made no pauses for photography and we were even quite glad of simpler going once again when the rocks eventually petered out on a slope of sandy scree.

We felt the cold still more beyond the summit, when we tried to shelter from a furious squall of rain. Huddled in a shallow rock-scoop, we did our best to keep as dry and warm as we could, while the shower hissed spitefully across the screes. But we had only slight protection and we looked out forlornly on a world from which all colour had gone. Indeed, the contrast between this wretched foxhole and our delectable sun-trap of so shortly before could scarcely have been sharper and it was difficult not to let our morale slip into a decline. It would have been easy enough at this point to call it a day and make tracks downhill to the bothy and our tent.

There was, however, no chance of such a simple way out as that. Honour had yet to be satisfied. On the programme there still remained the third and fourth of our 'Munros': Mullach Coire Mhic Fhearchair, 'the top of the corrie of the son of Farquhar', and Sgurr Ban, 'the white peak'. Having come thus far we could not possibly contemplate failing to 'bag' them both. However wet, however weary, we would keep each other company to the bitter end.

A deer-track scarring a black scowl of cliff took us upwards at a slant, high over a sunless corrie. The rocks above, mossgrown and dripping, seemed poised to thrust us outwards over the fretted edge of the path. Even across the more expansive boulder-carpet below, the outlook was sombre and unfriendly.

But the weather was mending yet again on this extraordinary day of many changes. The clouds were scattering on the wind once more, leaving rents and tatters of blue. The gale scouring the col felt less damp on our cheeks, and although on the upper slopes of Mullach Coire Mhic Fhearchair the mist was still driving like smoke over the slats and slabs of the scree, there was more than a hint of returning warmth. So too on the dip and lift beyond—the steep drop from the 3,326-foot Mullach, highest of our day's summits, and the giant's stairway to Sgurr Ban—the sky was steadily brightening. We topped the last rise to a plateau of dazzling white quartzite and there stood the cairn, the final goal, set against pools of blue sky and majestic white cumulus.

Theo, first there as usual, was quickly ensconced in an arm-chair of quartzite chunks. "Try a sandwich?" he queried, holding out an impressive-looking pile of doorsteps. "No pemmican fillings, only strawberry jam."

I accepted his offer, but with rather dubious enthusiasm. It had to be admitted that I was rapidly approaching that state of weariness when eating anything more substantial than boiled sweets is itself quite a feat of endurance. I had already started to rely rather ominously on that wonderful energiser, vitaglucose, thinking long thoughts the while of endless mugs of warm, sweet tea. And now, as we sat at the last cairn of the day, my morale was shaken even further by the full realisation of our situation: not only were we almost as far away from base as we had been at the top of A'Mhaighdean, but the whole mass of the Mullach lay directly astride our homeward way. However desperately I searched the map, I could find no com-forting answer.

"I reckon that's our best route over there," commented Theo, indicating a scree-face of sickening steepness leading up to the Mullach's south-eastern ridge. "Once above that it'll be downhill all the way."

It was no good pretending not to hear, or even showing a sudden lively interest in the far maze of the Sutherland hills. The facts had to be faced. In desperation I tried out an argu-ment in favour of a low-level traverse westwards, but it all sounded pitifully thin and weak. In short, it was obvious from the start that I was lost.

Half an hour later we were fairly committed to the scree-face. Boots scratted and jarred on the crunching, sliding blocks; now and again smaller stones went scuttering and bounding from beneath our feet; sometimes we stumbled and swayed, maddeningly out of balance, until I began to imagine myself as ungainly as one of Hannibal's elephants in the Alps. Sheltered in our rock-bowl from the wind, we grew hotter and hotter and hotter.

But scree-faces—as well we knew—are never as steep as they look, and our long upward traverse ended at last on the ridge. We topped the crest near a minor summit and paused once again to draw breath.

Round and below us stretched the gayest views of the day. The wind had scoured the sky clear at last and the evening sun, shining free, added a kindlier warmth to the colours, from nearest rocks to horizon rim. Past the quartzite cap of Sgurr Ban, a ragged desolation of hills and glens reached away to the north-east; nearer jostled the friendly company of the Fannichs, at their side the outlier Fionn Bheinn, and now ahead of us lay outspread the patchwork browns of moorland across which led our way to the bothy. We went down. In a few minutes we were far below the ridge-crest.

A fine scree-run speeded us on our way, a ribbon of soft red earth and small stones that we raced down with cheerful abandon; and our pace would have been faster still if only our knees had been less stiff with the day's miles. Then we were down once again on the moor, resuming the old familiar struggle with its pitiless folds and furrows. In a few moments our swoop was forgotten; only hard work had reality. As we laboured through the thick heather, I began to feel I must be looking singularly like the Palmer, face to face with Marmion in the castle hall:

> But his gaunt frame was worn with toil;
> His cheek was sunk, alas the while!
> And when he struggled at a smile,
> His eye look'd haggard wild.

This stretch lasted for no more than 2 miles, although it seemed to me like 10. Soon I was picturing the path from Lochan Fada as the end of all our tribulations. But as Jimmy Swan, the commercial traveller, aptly put it: "No man's hame for the nicht until he has aff his boots," and the track, when I reached it, appeared to have twice as many switchbacks as it had in the morning. Every now and again I sat down and the rests grew longer and longer. Even vitaglucose failed to make my conscience respond to the shameful realisation that Theo must be already back at the bothy, no doubt hard at work getting supper.

My conscience was only too right. I poked my head through the ruined doorway and there was the primus roaring at full blast, with Theo crouched like a troll over a thick brew of mushroom soup. As I shed my rucksack on the floor, he reached me up a welcoming dram which he had had in readiness. I was not slow to accept it; even Dandie Dinmont would have agreed that it was "a gey stiff cheerer". Then I sat down contentedly on the end of a rickety bench. The time, I noticed, was 10.15. We had been out exactly twelve hours.

Despite our weariness supper that evening tasted particularly good. We talked little, half listening to the songs of the meadow-pipits as we watched the slow advance of darkness over the great wide sea of the heather. The day's reminiscences would keep till later and be all the better for that.

Next morning we were away at 8.30, each of us, like Modestine, burdened with a "monstrous deck-cargo". Summer seemed to have come overnight in a single stride. There was a softness in the breeze far different from the occasional icy buffetings of the previous day; gay colours everywhere, from the brown trout-pools of the burn to the smoky blue shoulder of Slioch, danced in the early light. Now and again wheatears flew off to chatter at us from nearby boulders, and downstream from a waterfall a pair of dippers sped away with nervous bobbing and curtsying, well out of harm's way.

Much to our surprise we came on a young man comfortably couched on a heathery knoll—the first person we had seen for almost forty-eight hours. He proved to be a bird-watcher, a fervid enthusiast who had come all the way from Bradford on his motor-cycle to look for golden eagles. So far his search had been unsuccessful, but as we talked, he had his telescope trained on a pair of black-throated divers out on a lochan. We wondered if the rewards of his brief week-end in Wester Ross would be compensation enough for all his trouble.

There was no need to hurry, but even so we made fast time along the sandy track and soon we were stopping for a last look back at the hills. There stretched the now familiar outline, from A'Mhaighdean the whole way along to the black pinnacles of the Mullach. For a little we let fancy idle over the sequence of barren tops, watching the play of golden light as the sun gained in power.

Then, heaving our rucksacks to our shoulders once more, we dropped down into the bowl of Gleann na Muice.

6

The Islands

The shores of Mull on the eastward lay
And Ulva dark and Colonsay,
And all the group of islets gay
That guard famed Staffa round.

Sir Walter Scott

IN an immense ragged crescent, the west coast of the island of
Mull sweeps round from Calgary Bay in the north to the Ross
of Mull and Iona in the south. Half way across the entrance,
like a string of beads, stretch the Treshnish Isles—Carn a'
Burg Mor and Carn a' Burg Beag, Fladda, Lunga and the
Dutchman's Cap; inside cluster another half dozen islands—
Ulva and Gometra, Eorsa and Inchkenneth, Little Colonsay
and Staffa—each with its attendant outliers. Backed by lonely
cliffs and hills, the archipelago makes one of the most fascinating
sections of the whole Scottish coastline.

Twice—in August 1943 and in May 1946—I had the good
fortune to look down on the islands; ravens' eye views from
the summit cairn of Ben More, highest of the Mull hills. This
double introduction was followed not long afterwards by two
unsuccessful attempts to reach Staffa and first acquaintance
instead with Iona, but it was not until 1963 that I managed
to carry out a plan which had been clamouring for attention
for some time: the paying of a quick visit to Ulva, largest of
these satellite islands of Mull.

Leisure unfortunately was limited. A single day was all that
could be spared, a fact which posed something of a problem,
as it was still the summer before the introduction of the island
car-ferries. There was one outward passenger sailing from
Oban to Mull at nine o'clock every morning, but it was
only on Thursday evenings that the MacBrayne timetable
conceded a late steamer back from Tobermory to Oban. Just
once a week, then, there was the chance to enjoy a really full
day on Mull.

Self-portrait and basalt pillar, Ulva

I left Glasgow by car at six o'clock on a perfect June morning. The radiance of the early sunshine quickly wiped out the memory of jangling alarm-clock and scanty breakfast. Up Loch Lomondside into Glen Falloch, through the suntrap of Glen Lochy, down beside the umber and yellow tide-wrack of Loch Etive the heat grew steadily. And there, reaching to horizons already vague in haze, lay the Firth of Lorne still and untroubled under a brazen sky.

The *King George V* slipped out of Oban Bay to meet only the laziest of swells. Even off Lady Rock the tide-jabble could barely be felt as we passed between it and Lismore into the mirror calm of the Sound of Mull. As I disembarked at Tobermory and watched the *King George V* swing away again from the pier to continue her run north-about round Mull to Staffa and Iona, it was impossible not to feel envious of the passengers still on board. The thought of the day of ease which lay before them made any kind of effort ashore seem singularly unattractive by comparison.

Main Street, Tobermory, gave back the heat like the inner lining of a baking-tin. Here and there above the roadway the air was beginning to dance and shimmer in mirage-pools of quicksilver. Already the day promised to break all previous records of a sweltering midsummer week.

Unfortunately the day's work had to start sometime. Shouldering my pessimistically heavy rucksack, I set off to claim the bicycle which I had previously arranged to hire for the day.

My expectations could not have been said to be high: cycling on Mull has always seemed to me to plumb depths of wretchedness utterly unknown elsewhere. I proceeded to the back of the shop in the wake of the owner much as one might have accepted an invitation to inspect the tumbril that was to transport one to the guillotine.

"Where are you bound for?" asked my companion brightly, producing the machine on which the day's destiny was to hang. I noticed with some satisfaction that it had the traditional two wheels and handlebars, also a saddle of sorts. No doubt the snags would show themselves later on.

"Dervaig," I replied, "then, if possible, over to Ulva. Why?" A momentary shadow seemed to have crossed his face.

Columnar basalt, Ulva. Mull in the background

"Nothing really. I was only wondering if you knew the Dervaig road. The hills on it, I mean. They're worth treating with a bit of respect, you know. Just the other day there we had a couple of girl visitors from Dervaig on their bicycles and one of them went over the handlebars and stunned herself."

I commiserated rather wanly. A certain amount of pessimism, it seemed, was warranted.

To begin with, however, there was little actual danger: it was impossible to cycle at all. The road climbed steeply, interminably upwards, at first shut in, but twisting higher through the outskirts of the town. All one could do was trudge slowly uphill, yard after dusty yard; it seemed a mere mockery to have to push a bicycle as well. Then, at length, the trees thinned and the last of the houses was left behind. The air freshened, the outlook widened, and the road, after a final defiant lift, began to level off more charitably. Clearly the time had come to mount; there was nothing for it but to grit the teeth and get on with it, like Macbeth:

> "I am settled, and bend up each corporal agent to this terrible feat."

The expedition plan was to make the day's cycling into a circular tour—first, by way of Mr. George Scott-Moncrieff's "high, switchbacking, twisting, exhilarating road" to Dervaig and thence by Torloisk to the Ulva Ferry; then back, on a less exalted level, along the shore of Loch na Keal and through Salen: a grand total of 34 miles. Except for the 3 miles approaching Salen on the return run, the whole of this round would be new to me, although the country through which it passed had become familiar enough in my distant views. One thing at least should be certain: there would be no lack of interest in the scenery.

Meanwhile the first part of the journey—the 7-mile stretch to Dervaig—was already demanding serious attention. In particular it was necessary to re-learn the old lesson that suddenly having to start pedalling a bicycle after years of abstinence and without any previous training is a good deal less pleasant than facing the same bit of road from behind the steering wheel of a car.

Not that there was any excuse for grumbling so far as weather and views were concerned. It was a peerless morning, still young and fresh, and gay with the exhilaration of June at its best. Larks and meadow-pipits exulted in an outpouring of song, accompanied rather less musically by the restless clacking of wheatears and an occasional stonechat. The sun even seemed to have drawn from the surrounding moorland a double measure of that heady compound of scents, so completely indefinable and essentially Highland—bog myrtle and young heather and invading bracken shoots.

The narrow, curving Mishnish Lochs, which border the road for close on 2 miles, had a royalty in their blueness that I had forgotten existed anywhere south of Sutherland. So brilliant, too, was the green of their banks that the sudden vividness of colouring was almost startling. From a white shingle spit a pair of sandpipers took flight, piping anxiously as they skimmed the loch-fringe. Here the going was more level and much pleasanter in consequence. Indeed almost before I had realised it, I had reached the far end. This was fully half way to Dervaig and an excellent excuse for a halt, so I dismounted and sat back luxuriously, shoulders propped against a dusty bank where thyme and ling sprawled.

The chain of the three Mishnish Lochs lies at an altitude of almost 500 feet and it is from the west end of their moorland saucer that the road takes its first plunge. It seemed a delightful change, of course, to be starting to freewheel at last, but in less than 100 yards it became alarmingly clear that this was no more than an irony of fate: quite suddenly the gradient was so fierce, the surface so loose, the cornering so violent, that I had to clutch wildly at the brakes, hoping fervently that I might escape being pitched head over handlebars into the heather. On and on wound the descent, bend after loose gritty bend, and on and on we bounced and juddered, the machine and I, brakes grating, teeth rattling, till I wondered if there would ever be any end to it all. Just when I was almost resigned to letting go and having one last dramatic gamble with gravity, the angle eased to a level stretch and it was possible to draw breath more normally. Death by stunning, swift, spectacular and final, had been avoided after all.

Having dropped the best part of 300 feet, the road flattened momentarily beside the head of little Loch an Torr. From a nearby bed of reeds a heron flew off, abandoning its morning fishing. Its slow, leisurely wing-beats seemed almost a reproof—a condemnation of every kind of haste and impatience and unnecessary work.

The bicycle and I eventually reached Dervaig a few minutes before midday, sustained by nothing other than the sheer perfection of the morning. We had mastered a second, seemingly endless ascent, a series of hairpin bends tilted wickedly upwards, and we had swooped and swung down the further side, the aerial views of the village a reassurance that the first part of the journey was coming to a successful conclusion. Seven hot miles lay behind and we were still up to schedule.

There was, that June morning, something about Dervaig reminiscent of one of the villages of the Austrian Tyrol. The dusty white ribbon of road dropping into it with such abruptness might well have been the descent from some high-altitude pass. Its clustered houses and gardens gave a first impression of peace and timelessness, for, with the exception of a solitary old man at work among his cabbages, there was no one about. Between its friendly flanking walls, bright in many places with flowers, the street stretched empty, trapping the sun. The only things missing in the glare and dancing dust were an onion-topped church tower and the fanciful colourings of beer garden awnings.

My spirits therefore were high as I went pedalling through the village. The most arduous part of the outward run was over and done with; soon now the first views of Mull's west coast would be coming up. Sun and scenery were combined in such perfection that I was very nearly tempted to risk a stave or two of one of the more popular songs. Benignly I smiled on a local heifer that raised an eyebrow at my passing from the far side of a fence.

Then suddenly, without warning, misfortune struck.

The bicycle juddered over a more ragged pothole than usual and a moment later the front tyre had gone as soft as pulp. We slowed to an anxious halt.

Now, of all the practical tasks at which I am almost uncannily useless the mending of bicycle punctures must surely top the list. Here, if anywhere, is an inescapable personal Waterloo. This was no exception. The preliminary ritual of

disembowelment having been carried through, it was discovered as usual that the inner tube was scarred and mottled
with a rash of patches, as though sorely stricken with measles.
There being no obvious hole, however, a bowl of water was
borrowed from a sympathetic housewife and the partially
inflated tube immersed. Nothing moved. Not a bubble rose
from the crystal depths of the water. It was left entirely to the
imagination to guess which of the spots looked thinnest. Then,
the most likely having been selected and patched, the tyre was
reassembled and put to the test.

If possible, it was flatter than before.

An hour and three-quarters later I found myself sitting back
luxuriously in one of Dervaig's two taxis, climbing the rutted
short-cut that curls over the hill to Torloisk. Much valuable
time had been squandered before this happy state of affairs
had been achieved, but now all the necessary arrangements
had been completed. I had eaten my lunch and had even made
big efforts to curb my impatience. The bicycle was out of
sight and almost out of mind, safe in the keeping of the village
blacksmith, whose nonchalant attitude to puncture-mending
was one to inspire the deepest admiration. The machine, he
assured me, would be ready waiting on my return later in the
afternoon. It was possible to face the future again with a
certain amount of optimism.

Quite suddenly, just past the watershed of our hill-road, the
islands came into view: Ulva and Gometra straight ahead, their
humped black masses surprisingly close and, against the sun,
magnified unnaturally by the surrounding dazzle of light; out
to sea the main chain of Treshnish—Fladda, Lunga, the
Dutchman's Cap—islands that are impossible to glimpse
without a catch at the breath. There they were again, inviting,
alluring, tantalising, withdrawn in the grey distance of the heat-
haze. Even if the day were to bring no further satisfaction, the
toil that lay behind would not have been in vain. This panorama
of well-known islands, as much perhaps as Ulva itself, was what
I had come to enjoy.

Not far from the junction of our track with the main road
we passed Torloisk House. Unobtrusive behind screening
trees, its name only just distinguishable on the half-inch map,
Torloisk is nevertheless a place of great interest. Before the

days of steamboats, and even for some time afterwards, it shared with Ulva the honour of being one of the jumping-off points for visitors to Staffa.

Towards the end of the eighteenth century a trip to Staffa was quite an undertaking. First one had to travel by fishing-smack from Oban to Aros, in Mull; then there was a walk, or more likely a ride on Highland pony-back, across the island to Torloisk or Ulva Ferry; finally, when the weather deigned to permit, there was the crossing by sailing boat of 9 miles of open sea. Small wonder if the whole arduous expedition sometimes took as long as ten days or a fortnight to accomplish.

It was from Torloisk that the famous French geologist and traveller, Faujas de Saint Fond, sailed out on his visit to Staffa in 1784, twelve years after the island's 'discovery' by Sir Joseph Banks. Saint Fond must have set off with a good deal of misgiving, for some of the other members of his party, eight in all with one day's provisions, had already been out to the island and had actually been storm-bound there for two days, living in incredible squalor with the local inhabitants—sixteen men, women and children, eight cows, one bull, twelve sheep, two horses, one pig, two dogs, one cock and eight hens. It is not recorded how far the livestock population was reduced in order to alleviate the visitors' pangs of hunger. For Saint Fond himself the sea was calmer and after a pleasantly full day on the island, the return to Torloisk was made in four and a half hours.

As we turned again along the sea-edge, we came in sight of. Ben More, looking remote and unreal in the haze. Its outline was barely distinguishable beyond Loch Tuath and the unseen arm of Loch na Keal and somehow this very vagueness suggested much more than its modest 3,169 feet, the vast frontage rather of some great mountain barrier leading back to far-distant snow-peaks capped by the clouds.

It was a pleasant 5 miles from Torloisk to the Ulva Ferry. After the short-cut over the moors the road seemed reasonable and sedate, its bordering trees remarkably profuse. Here and there hoodie crows were busy among the rocks and seaweed, and once, briefly, we glimpsed a fine waterfall, the Eas Fors, tumbling white down a deep black scimitar-gash in the cliffs.

In due course my rucksack and I were disgorged at the

ferry, the taxi-driver agreeing to return for me again at 5.30 p.m. Thanks to the puncture the time allowance for Ulva had been cut to a miserable shrunken fraction.

At the top of the slipway an enormous grocer's van was parked, its driver busy inside amid a bewilderment of stores. Close by the ferryman's wife was sitting enjoying the sunshine.

"Just over from the island doing the shopping," she remarked cheerfully as I shed my rucksack and took a seat on the concrete parapet. "My husband's across at the house but he'll be back on this side in a few minutes. I take it you're wanting over."

I admitted that that was my intention, then told how my time had been whittled down by ill luck. "And that, I'm afraid, means there's no chance of reaching Gometra too. I'm hoping all the same to have a look at the basaltic columns on Ulva; can you tell me the best way over to them?"

"Well, most people certainly like to go across to see the columns, but you won't need to waste any time. It's quite a distance. My husband will be able to tell you the road to take."

And so in due course he did, most helpfully, as we sat in the big broad-beamed ferry-boat, luxuriating in the warmth and watching the green water of the sound slipping quietly astern.

It is only some 200 yards from Mull across to Ulva; a sea-lane that is trifling, insignificant—and also thoroughly deceptive. Through its jaws and over its submerged reefs spin the tides between Loch Tuath and Loch na Keal; "a narrow intricate channel with many dangers", runs the official Admiralty description. Yet as we saw it nothing could have looked more innocent. Scarcely a ripple furrowed the water, smooth, cool, tempting. The sail was no more than a few minutes' blessed relaxation before work began again.

It was amusing to recall some of the illustrious travellers of the past who in their day had made this same island crossing. Boswell and Johnson, huddled in their cloaks against the harsh wind, making the passage in the long-boat of the Irish vessel *Bonnetta* on a pitch-black night of mid-October 1773. "It was the sixteenth of October," commented Johnson, "a time when it is not convenient to sleep in the Hebrides without a cover." James Hogg, the Ettrick Shepherd, visiting Staffa and Fingal's Cave and complaining in visitors' book doggerel of the greed of the local boatmen. Sir Walter Scott, outward bound on the first of his two visits to Staffa, crossing to Ulva with "colours flying and pipes playing" on a bright July day in 1810. He was to be the guest of the laird, Ranald MacDonald, and came ashore to a princely welcome accompanied by discharges of musketry and artillery.

My own landing had less obvious pomp and ceremony. As I shouldered my rucksack and walked off the slipway, the island seemed deserted, as lacking in interest in my arrival as the few idling gulls. The shore, the beginnings of a road, even the ferryman's cottage had apparently succumbed to the tyranny of afternoon heat. The only sound of any kind was the diminishing throb of the engine as the ferry-boat re-crossed the narrows to Mull.

With the rather forlorn hope of reaching Ulva's highest point, Beinn Chreagach (1,025 feet), I set off along the rough white road, its surface parched and dusty. At first it led across fairly open country, edged by clusters of foxgloves and flag irises. At one or two of the corners and forks, signposts pointed bleached wooden fingers to show the way to Gometra. Then followed a wooded stretch, thick higher up with larches and firs, and noisy at one point with the screeching and chatter of a heronry. I could have wished for the shade to last longer than it did for a little more help in maintaining a fast pace. But there was no justice: instead of rewarding honest toil the wood ended abruptly, giving place to open moorland where the sun at once resumed its merciless oppression. This was the butterfly zone, dozens of fritillaries and an occasional small tortoiseshell dancing ahead over the heather, while the number of blues I saw suggested the coast of Fife rather than Argyll. And again, most noticeably, there was the nostalgic scent of bog myrtle and ling.

The summit of Beinn Chreagach—if indeed it really was the summit that was visible—looked several miles away in the haze. It crowned ring upon ring of rounded basalt terraces, the whole formation, according to one guide-book writer, resembling the pyramids.

Somewhere beyond lay Gometra. With more time available it would have been quite accessible, especially as a bridge spans the Bru, the narrow strait which separates it from Ulva. But even under ideal conditions such an addition to the programme would have meant a most strenuous afternoon; with the temperature soaring as it was, I was unashamedly glad it was out of the question.

There was no point therefore in following the road further, so I turned off on to the open hillside, making height steadily by a succession of helpful paths. Gradually the views opened out—on the one hand Loch Tuath, with its Mull background marked noticeably by the white scar of the Eas Fors; on the other the scattering of seaward islands, growing every moment into a more complicated design. And, behind, always the half-distinguishable mass of Ben More.

Quite soon it became obvious that there was no hope even for the last half mile to the top of Beinn Chreagach. With a detour to the south shore still in prospect, the 2 miles already covered in haste and in the heat of the day had been effort enough. I dumped my rucksack therefore and sat down. Then, having extricated a jam roll, squashed, sticky and completely delectable, I opened out the map to try and unravel the hopeless tangle of islands.

There must have been twenty of them at least, not counting the reefs and skerries and needles which dotted the network of channels. Farthest out was the Dutchman, unmistakable even at a hazy ten miles' range. Staffa, showing no distinctive features from this angle, lay beyond Little Colonsay with its 'big tower', the Torr Mor, while a crowd of lesser islets jostled for space in the restricted water between. Sprawled across the entrance to Loch na Keal was Inchkenneth, the island on which Dr. Johnson found the Sunday of his two-day visit "the most agreeable he had ever passed".

Surely this must be the most supremely satisfying area in Britain for the expert in sea-canoeing, an archipelago of intricate character and changing moods never likely to suffer from the contempt of too much familiarity. Little, perhaps, has been written about the pleasures to be enjoyed there, though that little makes them sound tempting enough. Compare, for example, the moods of two consecutive days as experienced by an outstanding master of the art of canoeing, Mr. J. Lewis Henderson:

Six miles of slow wandering brought us to the rocky islets

standing guard at the Sound of Ulva and we entered the narrows with a sense of pleasurable contrast. In place of limitless horizons, we had the nearness of friendly shores to bear us company. . . . Little bays and inlets dozed invitingly in the heat and into them we drifted, leaning overside to watch the variations in depth changing the tone of water from pale to deep green. The ripple of our movement sent dark oscillations of shadow creeping across the sandy bottom, above which, tiny fish would hang suspended in a kaleidoscope of cool colours.

And the next morning, crossing the open sea from the shelter of Ardmeanach to the Ross of Mull:

At the meeting, we struck and heeled to an invisible wall of wind. Breakers reared steeply, their crests a streaming rain of spindrift, their foaming descents a thing of power and menace against which we began the play of touch and go. It was make way in the troughs and out again before the next white comber charged upon us when, with noses dug deep and tails in the air, we would tear away downwind at a speed which raised our bow waves to fleering plumes and our wakes to broad swathes of creaming foam.*

As much, surely, as the most fastidious enthusiast could wish for.

My own way from the hog's back of Beinn Chreagach now lay down to Ulva's south shore. There seemed to be no paths at all on this side of the island and as the descent was for the most part diagonal, it cut tiresomely across the line of the gullies. Ulva is notorious for the prolific growth of its bracken— it is said to grow in places to heights which can easily hide all but the horns of the Highland cattle—and although it was too early in the summer for quite such luxuriance, I had to wallow and flounder often enough. On the airless lower ground, hurrying past the crumbled skeletons of old cottages overgrown with thistles and nettles and masses of buttercups, I grew hotter and hotter still. There was always the hope of finding a burn and this acted as a constant spur, but not a trickle was to be seen anywhere; each likely hollow in turn was as parched and thirsty as my throat, and even when I reached the sea's edge at last there was no consolation, as time was now too short for a swim.

It was not far along the shore to the first of the basaltic

* *Kayak to Cape Wrath*, by J. Lewis Henderson (William MacLellan, 1951).

outcrops—a low cliff, brown and wrinkled as a centenarian's face and gay at its base with clumps of bell heather. Beyond, on the farther arm of a small bay, stood two imposing rock-towers.

Dr. John Macculloch, that extraordinarily enterprising and energetic traveller who roamed the Highlands and islands in the days of the Prince Regent, commented aptly: "On the south-western shore of Ulva, the columnar rocks are often disposed in a very picturesque manner; being often broken, sometimes detached, and occasionally bearing a distant resemblance to ruined walls and towers. Had Ulva been the only basaltic island on this coast, it might possibly have attracted more attention; but it has been eclipsed by Staffa, and has remained unsung."

The turrets were strongly reminiscent of the rock-castle on the islet of Eilean na Cloiche, off Lismore. They had the same square-cut, vertical lines, the same smooth fluting, each upthrust from the tide's edge with the jut of a battle-cruiser's bow. Here the idler would need little persuasion indeed to seek out the ideal place for settling down and losing count of time.

A stone's throw beyond was a shallow grotto, lines of basalt pillars resting like organ-pipes on the wide arch of its roof. It was farther still, however, that I came on the best architecture of all: a small pebbled cove hemmed in by a high columnar wall. Here the pillars stood tall and regular, austerely straight and matched precisely for size. At the tip of the promontory they plunged, knife-edged, into the blue-green of the sea, a patch of white surf ringing their base. Comparisons with Staffa or the Shiant Isles would be profitless, yet in their own way, with their warm brown texture and capping of green grass set against the expanse of the sea and the background cliffs of Gribun, these fine columns made an impression that was quite remarkably vivid.

Time had moved swiftly since the pause up on the shoulder of Beinn Chreagach; Ulva's jealously reckoned ration of hours and minutes was almost at an end. It would have been pleasant to turn a few more corners of coastline, but now the temptation had to be resisted. There was no choice but to strike straight back to the ferry.

A herd of Highland cattle, gold and brown and absurdly shaggy for the day before midsummer, eyed me askance as I dived afresh into the bracken and started to struggle uphill once again. Immediately the green fronds clutched affectionately at my ankles, and every boulder and hole on the hillside seemed to have aligned itself directly in my path. Clearly it was to be a strenuous race against time.

A formal burial place, prominent on the top of a high hillock, would ordinarily have invited a visit, but now it had to be passed strongmindedly by. It was only possible to conjecture who lay buried there: some of the Clan MacQuarrie, maybe, whose ownership of Ulva is said to have lasted for 900 years; or possibly some of the MacArthurs, at one time famous for the college of piping which they conducted on the island. Whoever they may have been, the people who were brought here, they were given a matchless site for their last resting-place.

Not far beyond, Ulva House itself barred the way and called for a suitable detour, behind a screen of rhododendrons then through a hostile tangle of undergrowth. It was a relief to reach the road again and face the last white and dusty half mile to the ferry. On the far side of the sound I could see the car already waiting.

The outstanding event of the drive back to Dervaig was undoubtedly our stop at the schoolhouse. Here the kind lady who opened the door must surely have caught the glint of urgency in my eye, for without wasting time she hustled me through to the kitchen tap. Then, with growing incredulity, she watched while I made up for the aridity of Ulva. It was a moment when I would undoubtedly have subscribed to Para Handy's theory that "long life iss aal a maitter o' moisture".

As I relaxed in the taxi once again and watched the miles slipping by, I could not avoid a certain sneaking hope, faint it is true, but unworthy none the less—the hope that the Dervaig blacksmith had not been able to mend the puncture. If this were so then, of course, it would be possible to travel back in luxury and with a completely clear conscience the whole way to Tobermory, while the wretched bicycle was left to follow on by lorry the following morning. It was an agreeable speculation.

Unfortunately no sooner had we reached Dervaig hotel than

the hope was utterly shattered. There, propped up against the wall, was the machine itself, looking disgustingly fit, its tyres fairly exuding good health and vitality. Not the flimsiest excuse was left.

Perhaps in the heat and toil which followed it would have needed little persuasion to agree with Dr. Johnson's verdict on Mull: "A most dolorous country!" Yet in the end the 7 miles to Tobermory took little more than an hour. And eventually they had my spirits soaring again, for they finished in the exhilaration of a descent that was of just the right steepness and manageably smooth. As I dismounted and wheeled the machine into its stable, I felt that if—as I had vowed so many times during the trip—my cycling days really were over, at least they had enjoyed a thoroughly pleasant climax.

It was a perfect evening. The gold of the sun's rays, low-slanting now, struck across the blue of the bay to the barrier of Calve Island. The haze had gone; there was not a cloud in the sky; every colour glittered with a breath-taking clarity. Main Street was noisy with talk and laughter, friendly and gay, almost as if sensing the blessing of this incomparable June sundown.

Sailing-time was officially 8 p.m., but it was later than that before the masts of the *Lochnevis*, disembodied by the intervening green segment of Calve Island, could be seen moving ghostlike up the Sound of Mull. The passengers on board were on an evening cruise from Oban and it was a cheery throng that lined the rails as the steamer manoeuvred to the pier. The call was brief, the engine-room telegraph jangling restlessly till we were away, moving out across the bay past the stationary *Lochearn*, which had been lying off to leave more room. Soon Tobermory was lost to sight as we turned down the Sound.

I settled myself in comfort near the stern, the breeze quickly banishing memories of the day's oven-heat. Back towards the west the view was uninterrupted, the whole sky flaming with the sunset, dazzlingly, radiantly bright, and the steamer's wake making an unbroken avenue of gold into the very heart of the fire. Against the brilliance I watched the tireless retinue of gulls, endlessly planing and swaying to the air currents.

South, over Ben More, the white heat cooled, and later, far down the Firth of Lorne, the Isles of the Sea had already merged into the dove-grey background of twilight. But to west and north the afterglow never died. By its light Oban welcomed us back, and behind me, as I drove the last 90-mile lap back home to Glasgow, its radiance picked out one after another the silhouettes of familiar hills.

It is sometimes said that on Mull all roads lead to Iona. Certainly for us, after the start of the car-ferry between Oban and Craignure in 1964, the way across the island to the Iona ferry at Fionnphort became more and more familiar.

My own early experiences on Iona, of rain and mist and camping discomfort, were readily forgotten; in their place came a whole world of new impressions—of summer warmth and the scent of clover, of unceasing bird-song and almost unbelievable brilliance of colour. We camped at the North End and basked on the sands of Port Ban; we looked for Iona greenstones at St. Columba's Bay and we experienced again the peace and blessing of the abbey. Gradually we had added another vital piece to the build-up of the picture of Mull's western coastline.

Much remained, however: Erraid, for instance, off the very tip of the Ross; Staffa and its neighbours at the mouth of Loch na Keal; above all the distant string of the Treshnish Isles. Bac Mor, the Dutchman's Cap; Lunga, with the striking profile of Dun Cruit, the Harp Rock; Fladda; Carn a' Burg Mor and Carn a' Burg Beag—we knew the outlines of them all so well. If only the weather would play fair, Iona certainly seemed the ideal starting-point for the exposed 11-mile crossing to Lunga.

The opportunity came early on in the unpredictable summer of 1970. It had been our good fortune to choose a heatwave in June for a fortnight's holiday in Iona. The showers of the first week-end had gradually died away, and although the wind had veered to the east and remained strongly clamorous, each day had brought hotter and hotter sunshine. By our second Sunday the heat was almost cruelly brazen and the sea, for once, was mirror-calm.

For centuries Lunga and the Dutchman's Cap have been known for their good grazing for cattle; as long ago as 1549 they were both accorded honourable mention for this by Sir Donald Monro. They had, however, been given over to sheep

for a considerable number of years, until in 1969 Iona farmer
Gordon Grant tried the experiment of re-introducing cattle.
It was to have a look at these and to attend to the lambs that
our expedition was organised, two or three local helpers and a
happy band of more than a dozen holidaymakers crowding
into the big motor-boat belonging to Gordon's colleague in the
cattle enterprise, Alastair Gibson the Iona ferryman. I was
particularly glad to have with me David Forrest, who was
staying with us on Iona and renewing a long and affectionate
acquaintance with the island, but who had never previously
been out to the Treshnish.

It was late in the morning before we cast off from the jetty,
backing out past the thin screen of small craft at anchor. Soon
we were beyond the abbey and swinging through the gap
between the White Strand of the Monks and the jagged black
skerry-teeth of the Island of Storm. Gradually the familiar
outline of Dun-I merged into the grey haze astern.

On the way out to Lunga, which we reached in almost
exactly the predicted one and a half hours, the sea-birds were
'patchy'. At first, before we were well clear of Iona, we saw
numerous shags and terns, then, rather surprisingly, several
gannets. Farther out there were fulmars, puffins and a few
Manx shearwaters; somewhat unusually, I decided, the razorbills seemed to be outnumbering the guillemots. With the
morning still completely windless, the sea stretched round us in
oily calm, yet even so the surf was occasionally bursting white
along the cliff-defences of Staffa.

A landing on steep-to rocks with superb rough holds saw
most of the men, including the 'shepherds', ashore on Lunga.
The boat, with the women and children, was then to proceed
round the island to the anchorage at the north-west corner and
a later rendezvous there. As David and I climbed to the grassy
flats above, the sun beat on our backs with tropical ferocity;
we smelt the familiar, nostalgic, sea-bird island smell—that
compound of rank weeds, decaying seaweed and liberal
plasterings of guano—and against the background impreca-
tions of a whole army of herring gulls we heard the singing of
larks. Down below off the rocks, quite unconcerned, a black
guillemot was swimming idly. We could hardly have asked for
a better welcome.

The Treshnish Isles are of basalt, and both Lunga and the Dutchman's Cap rise centrally in volcanic cones, that of the latter being so conspicuous—like the crown of a wide-brimmed beaver—as to give it its striking name. The Cruachan, or 'haunch', of Lunga is 337 feet high, while the highest point of the Dutchman is 284 feet. Both, with their extensive rock-shelves, are well known as grey seal nurseries.

It was quickly apparent that the workers of the party had a really heavy day in front of them. Collecting the sheep and lambs was no simple task: the animals were not exactly co-operative and every gully, even every hollow had to be checked in the passing in case any were missed. On the other hand it was easy enough to be an onlooker, although the experts worked so fast and so tirelessly that there seemed to be all too few opportunities to hang back and use cameras or binoculars; one could have wished for unlimited time to savour this 'new' island to the full.

As we made our way across the grassy flats leading to the steep slopes of the Cruachan, larks and meadow-pipits accompanied us with an ecstatic outpouring of song. The occasional twites which we saw were rather less vocal; the black-backed gulls, both greater and lesser, and the oystercatchers decidedly less friendly. Then we were at the edge of the western cliff-rampart, looking down sheer, rugged walls to the erosion platform, over which streamed the restless surge of the Atlantic. At once we caught something of the vibrant, thrilling activity of the seabirds, an activity we were to be sensing more or less all the time we were on Lunga. One of our party was quickly away stalking the first trio of puffins with his camera; had he known how many better opportunities there were to be later in the day, he would probably not have bothered.

David and I walked on to have a closer look at Dun Cruit, the Harp Rock, which even at a distance gives such character to the west side of Lunga. Fronting the Atlantic with a sheer face 150 feet high, it is itself an islet cut off from the parent island by a narrow canyon-like channel. On a day of storm, with the great rollers striking hammer-blows on its wall, the rock must be a fine sight indeed. As we saw it, the whole place was at peace, the drowsiness emphasized by a company of shags along the cliff-edge, dozing in the midday warmth.

Dun Cruit, the Harp Rock, on Lunga,
Treshnish Isles

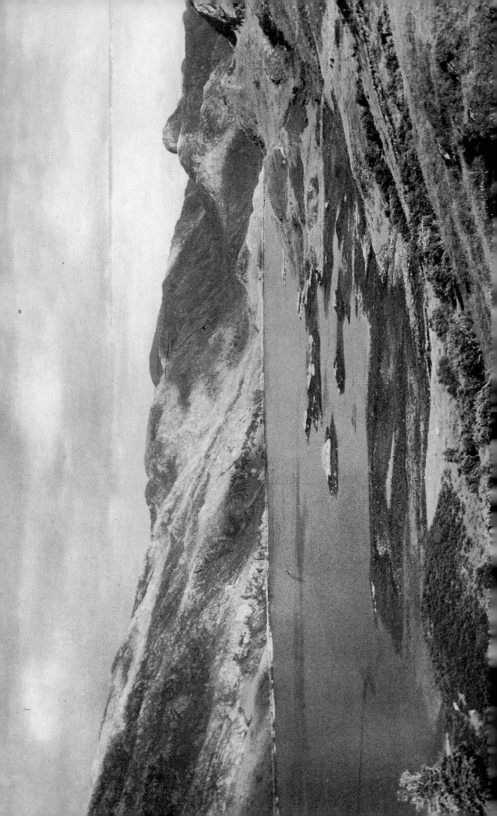

Behind us on the Cruachan there was a contrast of activity and noise as men and dogs toiled on with the sheep. The round-up goal was on the far side of the hill, where some of the island's ruined cottages are now made use of as sheep-fanks. Of course, with the perversity of their kind, the ewes took the most awkward routes they could find, so that progress over the hill looked uncommonly like the old familiar one pace forward and two paces back. In the blazing sunshine the running and the shouting and the endless doubling back must have been temper-trying to say the least.

A slender rickety cairn marks the highest point of the Cruachan. From here the round of views—almost entirely of islands—is matchless. For us there was too much haze, leaving Tiree and Coll, Rum and Eigg and Skye, even the rich details of Mull itself, largely to the imagination. But nearer at hand there was more than enough to satisfy. Previously I had always thought of the Treshnish as consisting of some half dozen individual and fair-sized islands; now as we saw them, looking north towards Fladda and Carn a' Burg Mor and Beag, the pattern was hopelessly confusing. The tide was fully out and the uncovering of reefs and skerries, teeth and islets, was complex beyond belief. All we could do was admire the colouring—chocolate and yellow and green against the silky spread of royal blue. Far below we could hear the lazy breaking of the waves, the perfect background accompaniment to the incessant singing of the larks.

Time was passing and a vast hunger for lunch was upon us. We sought out a grassy sun-trap and sat down to explore our packets of sandwiches. This was bliss indeed.

I was just fastening greedily on a hard-boiled egg of particularly tempting appearance when a fresh outbreak of shouting was borne in upon our ears. A couple of ewes and their lambs had broken back towards the succulent grazing they remembered from earlier in the day; there was no one within range to head them off. My conscience, I think, could have been stilled without any great difficulty; not so David's. In a moment he was on his feet and off across the slope to deal with the recalcitrant quartet. With less obvious zeal I followed in his wake. Ten minutes later we were back, warm and out of breath. We were just busying ourselves with the jam sandwich course when

Loch Glencoul, Sutherland,
a way of approach to Eas-Coul-Aulin

a ewe appeared on a distant skyline well behind the line of the advancing cordon. No one else had noticed her, I was certain. Surely, I reckoned, she deserved a blind eye. But no. Away we had to go again, up and down and round, till she too had been safely cornered. By then I suspect even David's conscience was becoming fractionally dulled. I did not wait, however, to find out, but packed up what remained of my lunch and sneaked away on an urgent quest for photographs.

Strangely enough, I had my reward. Down by the rim of the western cliffs were shags and puffins by the dozen; never before had I seen so many of either species concentrated so thickly. In a rock fissure, damp and sunless I came on a shag's nest with two scrawny, almost fully grown chicks in it. It was, however, the puffins which attracted me most, sitting rather foolishly beside their burrows or occasionally taking off for some fishing, with a display of vermilion legs and feet. I was amazed to find how tame they were and crept more than once to a range of no more than 5 feet.

Below the puffins, on the ledges of the cliff-face, there was a big scattering of nesting fulmars. Hereabouts, however, there were no kittiwakes to be seen; their preference appeared to be for the steep walls of Dun Cruit.

On a nearby extensive shelf of lush grass Gordon Grant's cattle were grazing contentedly. They did not look as though they had suffered in the least from their year of island exile; on the contrary they looked to be in excellent condition, their warm browns and blacks, against the more distant vivid blues and greens, making excellent material for colour photographs. They had, of course, been scrutinised already with a much more critical eye, and we learned afterwards that one of the herd had in fact been found dead at the foot of the cliffs—a loss of some seriousness. Two of the beasts had to be ferried across to Fladda and had been driven down to the flat rocks above the creek in which the motor-boat was lying. We arrived on the scene just as they were being pulled, pushed, coaxed and cajoled aboard—a task which seemed to require equal parts of strength and patience. Once they had been secured in the well of the boat, the animals looked reasonably happy, and there was evidently no need to have second thoughts about sharing the trip with them.

The passage to Fladda was quite remarkable. The straight-line distance from Lunga as the shag would fly is exactly one mile; our course must have been almost three times as far. From the creek we sailed south-west, directly away from Fladda, then swung west and north to skirt the islet outlier of Sgeir a' Chaisteil, 'the castle rock'. This looked encouraging but it was then necessary to turn in a complete semi-circle and face almost due south in order to pass through the fearsome maze of reefs we had looked down on so incredulously from the top of the Cruachan. Only after this obstacle had been cleared was it possible to turn due north once again, this time for the final 'leg' to Fladda. And for us the sea was in one of its most benevolent moods; it was June weather at its best. The eiders and black guillemots swimming idly in the inlets seemed to epitomise contentment. Yet it was only necessary to look a little more closely at the surroundings, at the reefs and rock-fangs almost within touching distance, to appreciate the potential dangers; in the tide surging and eddying over the shelves and round the skerries there was no mistaking the latent, menacing power. As Alastair Gibson commented afterwards when complimented on steering so tortuous a course without apparent difficulty: "I don't mind the channel on the flood tide, but it's a really nasty place on the ebb. It's mainly a question of memory, of course, though I'd be interested to take a look at it some day from a helicopter."

Fladda itself has no central cone like Lunga and the Dutchman; rather it is a plateau barely 50 feet above sea level and defended by sheer, fluted cliffs. We nosed into a poorly protected anchorage at the south-east corner and there, with further herculean pushings and pullings, managed to disembark the cattle. One of the beasts landed in the water, and I watched with some apprehension as it slithered and stumbled through the seaweed. Fortunately it avoided breaking a leg and the last we saw of it it had reached pastures new beyond the boulder beach, where peewits were crying their protests overhead.

It was disappointing that there was not enough time to cruise still farther round the northern outliers of the Treshnish. Close views of Carn a' Burg Mor and Carn a' Burg Beag, natural island strongholds with long histories, would have been especially memorable. Long ago these islands belonged in

turn to the MacDougalls and the MacLeans, and with their
daunting cliffs and swirling tide-rips must have been truly
impregnable before the days of heavy artillery. Even Martin
Martin, at the end of the seventeenth century, was able to
comment: "A very few men are able to defend these two forts
against a thousand. There is a small garrison of the standing
forces in them at present." The thick, loopholed wall which was
built to make attack still more difficult, as well as the ruins of
the fortress and chapel on the highest ground, may still be
seen on Carn a' Burg Mor.

The tide was flooding strongly as we sailed back to Lunga,
so that it was not necessary to run so far south before cutting
through to the western side. It was almost difficult now to
believe that the hostile world we had seen earlier in the
afternoon had ever existed. Even so there was much attractive
rock scenery, a score of towers and bastions and archways,
bright in the sunshine and each surmounted by its sentinel
shags.

The men who had remained on Lunga were still at work up
at the sheep-fanks when we arrived back at the creek. In the
relentless heat it must have been a particularly gruelling afternoon for them. At last, however, they were finished and we
watched them starting down the thread of a path past a spring
of ice-cold water, where two or three paused to drink. How
often in the past, I reflected, that same spring would be used
by the families who lived on the island. Theirs must have been
a hard, tough existence indeed and it is not surprising perhaps
that it should have come to a tragic end more than a century
ago, when apparently the little community was ravaged by a
severe epidemic.

It was six o'clock when we sailed once more, this time with
the full complement on board. Alastair set course only a short
distance out from the wall of Dun Cruit, then right down the
west side of Lunga, bound finally for the Dutchman. The gap
between the two islands is almost exactly 2 miles and as it
narrowed we looked ahead eagerly to yet another of the day's
scenic attractions. It was immensely impressive. Great steps
and scarps of basalt, grey and black and jagged against the
early evening sun, rose in a giant's staircase to the island's
crown. Soon we ourselves were in shadow, yet above us shafts

of sunlight came streaming over the shoulders of the hill as if through cathedral windows. It is said that the last person to live on the Dutchman was an outlaw; it would be difficult to imagine a lonelier place on which to suffer banishment.

Even on the calmest days the landing on Bac Mor has a bad reputation. It is no more than a shallow inlet, ill-protected, and with any size of a sea running the steep-to landing becomes tricky in the extreme. The swell when we arrived proved to be surprisingly heavy and it was decided that only the work party should land. They would be several hours yet, time enough for the remainder to be ferried back to Iona and for the motor-boat to return to the Dutchman once more. They lost little time jumping ashore on to a conveniently flat ledge, then, with barely a pause to wave us away, they were off uphill. We learned next day from Gordon Grant that they had not arrived back in Iona till after eleven o'clock.

The east wind had risen slightly, adding a new choppiness to the long slow swell rolling in from the Atlantic. Yet the heat seemed if anything to increase in intensity the nearer we came to Iona. The jetty was hot to the touch; the road round Martyrs Bay on the final stretch to the house hotter still. There was just time to turn round and hurry back with my wife to the Sunday evening service in the abbey. Inside there was coolness at last, coolness of flagstones and walls and vaulted ceiling, refreshing beyond words.

7

The Waterfall

And like a downward smoke, the slender stream
Along the cliff to fall and pause and fall did seem.

Tennyson

ONE pleasure which comes the way of most writers, either less or more often, is to receive letters from complete strangers, right out of the blue. Sometimes these letters are on the most unexpected subjects—and all the better for that; the surprises they contain have a way of doing more than simply breaking the monotony of the ordinary morning mail.

One such surprise was the letter which arrived from Mr. John Fielden, of Wilmslow, in Cheshire, back in the autumn of 1956. Mr. Fielden—according to the description he gave of himself—was a waterfall enthusiast. Not long before, he explained, he had happened on a magazine article of mine which had among its illustrations a photograph of a waterfall on Ben Hope, in Sutherland. Was this, he wondered, the same as Eas-Coul-Aulin, a fall which a guide-book he possessed described as the highest in Britain, higher even than the famous Falls of Glomach? He was keen to know, as he had it in mind to set out on a visit of discovery.

In one way the answer to John Fielden's query was not particularly important, for the Ben Hope waterfall was in fact relatively low. What did fire the imagination, however, was the realisation that somewhere in the Far North, in the most remote corner of the Scottish mainland, there was this obviously magnificent fall of which, admittedly, I had heard, but about which I knew virtually nothing. Somehow it was a fact which previously had never made the slightest impression.

Not indeed that anyone has ever troubled over much about the waterfalls of Scotland. Any Swiss, of course, would tell you at once of the magnificence of the Aar Gorge, or of the fantastic underground labyrinth of the Trümmelbach, near Lauterbrunnen. Any Icelander would extol Gullfoss and

Bruarfoss, Godafoss and Dettifoss; even his country's ships have been named after them. But the average Scot—much puzzled—would have the utmost difficulty in mentioning even half a dozen of his finest falls, let alone spelling their names correctly or pinpointing their locations on the map.

The enthusiasm which my English correspondent showed not only in his first but in numerous subsequent letters put me—and, by proxy, the majority of my fellow Scots—to shame. Writing later, in the summer of 1958, he told me that he had already visited some thirty-five different Scottish falls and had a list of over eighty more still to be seen—rather a formidable target, he and his wife had decided, for a forthcoming fortnight's holiday. Certainly there was no denying the impressiveness of a 'Top Fifty' table which ran like this: Acharn, Alltnacaillich, Ardessie, Avon, Barvick, Black, Braan, Bracklinn, Bruar, Cassley, Clyde, Conon, Corriemulzie, Cruachan, Divach, Dog, Dunrobin, Druim, Edinample, Eas-Coul-Aulin, Falloch, Fender, Foyers, Garaivalt, Glomach, Grey Mare's Tail, Keltie, Kilmorack, Kirkaig, Ledard, Leny, Leallt, Lochay, Meallt, Measach, Moness, Monzie, Morar, Mucomir, Muick, Plodda, Polldubh, Rogie, Shin, Steall, Tarf, Treig, Tummel, Turret, Victoria.

What interested me particularly, however, was the news that he had now actually carried out an expedition to Eas-Coul-Aulin along with four companions. From his description it was very evident that they had all been immensely impressed by what they had seen and would thoroughly recommend anyone else to follow their example. Apparently the exact location of the fall was 2 miles south-east of Loch na Gainmhich, 'the sandy loch', which lies close to the road over the hill from Inchnadamph to the ferry at Kylesku. Its waters dropped to the Amhainn an Loch Bhig, 'the river of the little loch', three-quarters of a mile from the head of the little loch itself, Loch Beag. On the one-inch Ordnance Survey map it was referred to as 'Waterfall'; no name, no red letters, no distinction at all; just quite simply 'Waterfall'. So much for publicity!

Meanwhile, although I had still not been stirred to action, my own curiosity had led to the gleaning of a little further information. For example, the road-book of one of the motoring organisations was found to have it on record that Eas-Coul-

Aulin was "considered by some authorities to be about thrice the height of Niagara when in full spate". Even allowing for the fact that Niagara's height is not its most noteworthy feature—a mere 167 feet on the American side—some simple arithmetic produced an intriguing total of just over 500 feet.

Again, in the Scottish Mountaineering Club's guidebook to *The Northern Highlands* I discovered: "On the south side of the valley, just three-quarters of a mile south-west of the Stack of Glencoul, the well-named Eas a' Chual Aluinn (Splendid Waterfall of Coul) falls over the open cliff-face from a height of 825 feet above sea-level. Its stream, which is about the size of the Glomach Burn of Kintail, falls some 500 feet (measured twice by aneroid) in three or four closely linked vertical leaps, and then steeply cascades another hundred and fifty." It was becoming more and more obvious that John Fielden's carefully assessed 570 feet was not far off the mark.

The heights of other falls also had taken on a new interest: the two plunges of the Falls of Foyers, on Loch Ness-side, together 205 feet; the well-known Falls of Measach, beside the road to Ullapool, a single drop of about 150 feet; and—always reputed previously to be Britain's highest at 370 feet—the Falls of Glomach. Overseas, the Victoria Falls could claim 360 feet; the Staubbach, in the Bernese Oberland, 980 feet; Gavarnie, in the Pyrenees, 1,385 feet. And highest in the world the Angel Falls in the mountains of eastern Venezuela, fifteen times as high as Niagara, their waters falling 3,212 feet, or more than half a mile, in a single sheet.

There was another fact too about Eas-Coul-Aulin which seemed to be becoming more and more evident as the weeks and months went by: slowly but very surely it was attracting wider attention. No doubt it was merely a question of time before some zealous planner, brilliant in his generation, decided that the water should be diverted from the fall and imprisoned in a hydro-electric pipeline. There were no two ways about it: a visit was called for before the sands ran out.

We chose a day in mid-July for the first of our ventures in waterfalling.

The expedition numbered four—my daughter Helen, son John, Lindley Carstairs and myself—and as we drove north from our holiday base on Speyside, our mood matched the gaiety of the early sun flashing across the eastern firths and on the great flat tableland of Ben Wyvis. There were rather more clouds on the move as we crossed the Sutherland border, but they still held no threat by the time we had passed Inchna-damph and forked right-handed at Skiag Bridge for the slow climb over towards Kylesku. Our luck with the weather at least seemed assured.

It is a desolate road that twists and crawls up to and over the watershed. On the left Quinag and on the right Glas Bheinn—tilted deserts of moor and shattered rock—seem to grudge the very existence of the thread between, with its occasional intruding cars. There are no buildings to be seen, not even any of the grey-walled Sutherland cottages that merge as if camou-flaged into the same grey of the background gneiss. It is the kind of country a man might run from—or travel uncounted miles to visit over and over again and absorb into the very fibre of his being.

Our starting-point, with the car parked in a thin wedge of a passing-place, was the '788' spot-height on the half-inch Bartholomew. Just below, in a saucer of heather and polished rock-slabs, lay Loch na Gainmhich. Its water caught the sun, though the sky was not sufficiently cloud-free to allow it that incredible royal blue which so often characterises the lochs of Sutherland. The line we chose across the moor was towards a crescent of shingle skirting the lochan's southern tip.

A sudden sharp howl proclaimed that our vanguard was fairly into the heather. John had been bitten by a cleg.

The insects must have seen us coming, for they came flying in from every direction, marshalling their squadrons among the bog myrtle and peat-furrows, ready for silent onslaughts as soon as we trailed past. The attacks were vicious while they lasted, but petered out as soon as we began to climb beyond the lochan, now on a path that zigzagged steeply between a couple of noisy burns. Here we toiled upwards, warmly but without difficulty, the only untoward incident occurring when my daughter decided to fall into a waterfall pool, to emerge dripping and surprised like a circus seal from its tank.

Behind us, Quinag began to disclose the whole complex pattern of its eastern walls—switchback ridges and arid corries swinging round to the long, arrogant nose of Sail Gharbh. It is roughly the profile of the latter that makes the Barrel Buttress, that stupendous, airy "hogshead, hooped and coopered at the middle", which, more than fifty years ago, Raeburn, Ling and Mackay were the first to climb in six hours of exhilarating rock-work. My gaze roved up and down the staves of the great barrel as we sat down beside a boulder for a five-minute rest. The distance was too far for detail, but imagination filled in the features of the route—the central 'belly-band' with its sensational corridor, the tottery flakes of rock, and the delicate holds with nothing but fresh air between boot-soles and heather, 300 feet beneath.

North of Quinag was the sea, with that complicated pattern of coastline framing Eddrachillis Bay and the mouth of Loch Cairnbawn—countless inlets and islets, like a scattering of jigsaw pieces, where once more imagination went wandering.

On our way once again, we eventually reached the skyline, climbing out to a bare plateau beyond a deep-cupped lochan where a solitary red-throated diver was swimming. We stopped, eager to see what lay ahead.

"Well, the path still looks obvious enough," remarked Lindley cheerfully. "Someone's done a useful job blazing the trail for us." The route showed grey in intermittent scars across the face of heather and rock-slabs. Here and there a stone or two had been scraped together into a diminutive cairn. Certainly there seemed to be no excuse as yet for losing ourselves irretrievably.

Fifteen hundred feet below and at right angles to our line of approach lay the trench of the Amhainn an Loch Bhig. This was the river into which Eas-Coul-Aulin dropped, but as the fall was in the dead ground falling away from our feet on our own side of the glen, it was still completely hidden. As if in rivalry, however, a chain of waterfalls streaked the hillside opposite from top to bottom like a tenuous white vein.

Some fifteen minutes later we reached the main stream eventually forming Eas-Coul-Aulin itself. This is fed from the east flank of Glas Bheinn (2,541 feet), draining an extraordinarily complex network of smaller burns and lochans. According to the map our path crossed the stream at a point about half a mile from the lip of the fall, then continued on, pleasantly enough but rather unhelpfully, parallel to the edge of the cliffs. We had to leave it therefore and fight our way down beside the stream through a jungle of deep heather and hidden rocks. The going was decidedly laborious, but we were kept from flagging by the realisation that we had almost reached our goal. At length the angle eased. We stepped out on to a kinder, more level plateau. A green-brown moorland strip led in a score or so of yards to the rocks at the cliff-top.

On our left the burn checked for a moment in a pool of quiet brown eddies as if to draw breath before the violence of its plunge.

As we walked forward, the first murmurs we had heard grew to a muttering, then to a louder, more insistent grumble. Suddenly we were at the lip, watching, to a wild accompaniment of thunder, the whole white fall spilling and spurting outwards in its long drop to the glen.

For many minutes we stood as if hypnotised. The burn was not in spate, yet immediately as it shot into space, the volume of water seemed to increase immeasurably, to gain an explosive force which carried it far out from the cliff-face. The eye would follow a single jet, see it leap from the take-off and hang seemingly motionless, suspended in mid-air, till in a flash it was snatched back into bursting spume, where rock-fangs thrust outwards from a shelf, far below. In the fantastic white cataract, foaming and flashing in its tempestuous plunge, stark ferocity was closely allied to beauty.

Behind the line of the fall, the cliffs bent round and merged into the steep background slopes of Cnoc na Creige. On the floor of the glen the Amhainn an Loch Bhig wound its last half mile to the tidal waters of Loch Beag. As we watched, sunshine and cloud kept changing the patterns of greens and blues and all-pervasive greys. The setting was fitting indeed for 'the splendid waterfall of Coul'.

We turned to the more prosaic consideration of sandwich lunch. Then, after a few parting glimpses from the cliff-edge eyrie, we started the long walk back—to the friendly path and the zigzags to the col; down the far side again into the afternoon sun, aslant past the shingle of Loch na Gainmhich. By the time we had emerged on to the moor of the clegs, our repertoire of marching songs was at an end and we had started on dirges.

"The Bonnie Earl o' Moray"—fifth time through—saw us eventually to the car.

During the months which followed, our thoughts often went back to that July day and our visit to Eas-Coul-Aulin.

Thanks in part to the weather, our plans had gone smoothly and well. We had enjoyed a grand day in a new bit of country. Indeed it had all been a worthwhile climax to the story which John Fielden's letter had started three years before. We had every reason to sit back and bask in a pleasant glow of satisfaction. Except for one nagging regret—we had only seen the fall from above.

The more we thought about it, the more we realised how unfortunate this was. Obviously no waterfall of any size could possibly be appreciated, let alone measured, unless examined from more than one point of vantage. As well suggest that the North Wall of the Eiger gives the same impression of immensity when studied from the hotel terrace at Kleine Scheidegg as it does when seen by a climber on the life and death toe-holds of 'The Spider' 5,000 feet above.

There was, in short, only one thing to be done: we must go back and have another look.

The lazy way of approaching Eas-Coul-Aulin is by boat. From the sea, Loch Cairnbawn runs inland for almost 4 miles to the narrows at Kylesku Ferry. Another mile farther on this splendid fjord divides to form Loch Glendhu and the more southerly arm, Loch Glencoul, the latter shrinking at its head into the little inlet of Loch Beag. If one could reach the southern tip of Loch Beag—a sail of a fraction over 4 miles from Kylesku—it would be no more than a stroll up the glen to the foot of Eas-Coul-Aulin.

This was, of course, the approach-route we had looked down on from our eyrie at the lip of the fall. The answer could not have been simpler: all we needed was a boat.

In the event it proved to be so difficult that, even with a whole Sutherland summer holiday at our disposal, we had to admit failure.

At Kylesku itself we had no luck at all. Nothing with a motor in it was available for public use; there appeared to be no two ways about that. There was the possible alternative of a rowing-boat, but it had to be admitted that, whatever the scenic attractions of Loch Glencoul, they seemed barely adequate compensation for nearly 9 miles of toil at the oars.

"You'd best try Jimmy the boatman," we were advised at our holiday base in Stoer. "Jimmy would take you, no doubt about that."

"And how can we get in touch with Jimmy?" we asked hopefully. "He wouldn't be on the phone by any chance?"

That was too easy a way out.

"Jimmy lives a wee bittie from the road," we were told. "Maybe about 2 or 3 miles. You could be asking the postie at Drumbeg now to take a message for you."

The idea was attractive. But holiday fortnights have a way of waiting for no man, not even a kindly Sutherland postman. We went to find Jimmy for ourselves.

At the second attempt, after fighting our way through birch scrub and bracken, across seas of bog and past a barrier screen of rock bluffs, we succeeded. Jimmy fortunately was at home, busy about his cottage with its minute garden facing across a crescent of shingle to the blue of Loch Cairnbawn. After some discussion we managed to fix a day for the waterfall venture, starting after breakfast from Kylesku and ending early enough in the afternoon to let Jimmy attend to his fishing. It looked as though our hopes were to be realised at last.

But it was not to be. Our luck seemed to have vanished after all. The day we had chosen proved to be the worst of the whole holiday.

We wakened to a tearing gale and rain that rattled like shot on the windows. Campers and caravanners down by the beach had spent a night of misery, as the wind screamed at them through the cannonade of the waves and the blatters of flying spindrift. In the lee of the point gulls and oystercatchers sought shelter from the flailing gusts, and farther out, in the inlets between the reefs, families of eiders swam within feet of boiling surf-cauldrons. Endlessly, monotonously, the grey waves hurried shorewards to cascade over the rocks in explosive bursts of white. So much for the holiday weather of July.

From the first it was clear that the boat journey was out of the question. A phone-call to Kylesku gave confirmation: there was no sign of our boatman and it was obvious that he would be storm-bound. The ferry itself had not been able to make a single crossing.

We were reluctant to give up our plan, to admit defeat and disappointment. But the weather gave no promise of better things, and a second trek to discuss new ways and means with Jimmy would almost certainly have been a waste of time. Already the holiday was passing with disturbing speed. So far as motor-boating was concerned, we could do no more than start looking forward rather enviously to some vague occasion in the future when good luck and good planning might be persuaded to coincide.

During the days that followed there seemed to be no respite from leaden skies and drizzle, no escape from the cold hostility of the wind. Mist blanked out Canisp and Suilven and Stack Polly, even, at times, the grey gneiss hillock just across the road from our house in Stoer. In Scourie they told us it was the worst summer they had known for thirty-five years.

Fortunately there was one great consolation—the wetter it was the more spectacular Eas-Coul-Aulin itself would be. There certainly was no excuse for sitting huddled against the cold in front of our peat fire. After all, we decided, the true, dyed-in-the-wool waterfaller should be at his happiest when it was pouring cats and dogs; like the Wet Man of Muscadale, he should be "the wan man in Scotland ye would find lamentin' if it wassna rainin' ".

We made ready, therefore, for a return visit to Eas-Coul-Aulin, once again by the overland route. With the burn angry in spate and an approach duly varied to provide a completely new viewpoint, this would be no mere second best to the sail up Loch Glencoul. The longer we thought about it, the higher our hopes soared.

There was certainly no pessimism in evidence in the hilarious car-load that swung and bounced along the Loch Assynt road to Skiag Bridge. Helen and John had been joined by two boys from Cumberland, Nigel Freeman and Bobby Key, both fast goers already used to the Lake District fells. The quinquagenarian apart, the average age of the party was just 15.

"Come on, old timer, what's the delay?"

"Hey! What's holding you back now? A pity we forgot your wheelchair!"

The disrespectful sallies would fly thick and fast; well I knew it. Until the hard work began.

Behind us, as we crossed the moor, mist was seeping into each fold and furrow of Quinag's eastern flanks, curtaining entirely the higher pattern of the ridges. Loch na Gainmhich, in its hollow, was hardly touched by the wind, although now and again we felt a smirr of rain on our cheeks, strengthening the pervasive scent of the bog myrtle.

But damp and warm though it was, we made short work of the climb to the pass. In many places the track had become no better than a stream-bed, frothing with peat-stained water.

"Imagine this being the path to Switzerland's highest waterfall!" laughed Helen, extricating herself from one of the flanking morasses. "The local *Kurverein* would need to do something about it if they wanted to keep their jobs."

I shuddered. The idea of any kind of commercialisation on these quiet hills did not bear thinking about. I had to thrust aside a sudden mental picture of thronged souvenir shops, of ticket offices and, outside, of uniformed menials with solemn faces and long-handled shovels, busy scooping up all the roughest stones from the path. No; rather let us go on suffering our rain, our bogs, our midges and all the other discomforts, with the most profound thanks that they are still as they are.

Our plan this time was to resist the temptation of leaving the track too soon in order to take the elusive short-cut to the lip of the waterfall. Instead, we would keep on for at least a further half mile, hoping then to be able to work down through the cliff defences of the glen. In due course this detour should bring us, 1,500 feet below the pass, to the foot of the fall itself.

Mist still clung obstinately round the desolation of Glas Bheinn's slabs and screes, high on our right; directly ahead, beyond the trough of the glen, it eddied listlessly about the great battleship prow of the Stack of Glencoul and its neighbouring thread of waterfall. The latter foamed white in spate and it was not surprising that Nigel immediately took it to be Eas-Coul-Aulin; we wondered how many other visitors must have made the same mistake. Lower down we found crossing the burn to be an unexpectedly tricky business; on the other hand, the actual wall of the glen presented no problem at all, merely slowing us down with a stretch of tiresomely steep grass.

A herd of deer, fifty strong, moved off at our approach, much to the delight of the English boys, who had never seen any before.

Helen and Nigel were first on the floor of the glen. On the near side of the river, the familiar Amhainn an Loch Bhig, they found a switchback sheep-track running back under the cliffs through a wilderness of fallen rocks.

"There it is," came their elated shout a few minutes later. "It looks great from here. Come on and see it."

Round a jagged rock-corner we saw the fall, dropping from incredibly high above, purest white against the black and green of its sheer background wall.

As expected, the recent rain had given it a new magnificence. It was very obviously more impressive than when we had seen it before, with an immense volume of water funnelling through the needle's eye slit at the cliff-top. Bursting free, long jets seemed to hang suspended in mid-air, stressing vividly the impression of height. Then, as they exploded on the outthrust rocks far below, a fine mist of spray drifted slowly away down wind. Burst after shattering burst we watched, although so high were they above us that not a sound reached our ears. Here was a replica of the poet's land of fantasy, where

> . . . the long waterfalls
> Pour'd in a thunderless plunge to the base of the mountain walls.

A plaintive reminder about lunch brought my thoughts back to a more mundane level. It was already after 1.30 p.m.

We sat down facing the fall, our backs against a giant block of gneiss. As if to bid us welcome, the sky lightened for the first time and we saw a few thin tatters of blue. Down the glen the sun was making brave efforts to burst through. Occasional bright patches on the hillsides and along the green edges of the river made me think all the more enviously of the boat-trip we had missed. The details were so easy to picture: the start from Kylesku, with the tide streaming fast through the narrows and the loch dazzling in morning sunlight; terns at their breakfast fishing; on one of the skylines, maybe, a few hinds grazing; ahead the Stack of Glencoul, dominant as a medieval German *Schloss* high above the Rhine; and finally the mile on foot by the Amhainn an Loch Bhig, the route we could now see

Eas-Coul-Aulin seen from the glen at its foot

so well climbing amiably towards us from the head of the loch. A journey undoubtedly for the connoisseur.

The only other approach-route at all worthy of consideration appears to have very much less to commend it. From the Kylesku road near Unapool House it follows the line of Loch Glencoul right round into the waterfall glen. There is, however, no path, and at one point some 200 feet above the loch it is necessary to cross a slope of dauntingly steep grass above a cliff face. As the Scottish Mountaineering Club guide-book pertinently remarks: "In wind and rain, with an ill-equipped party, this can be awkward."

I tried to figure out where this 'bad step' must be, but it was impossible to decide with certainty; somewhere, probably, on the slopes of Cnoc na Creige which, over a mile away, plunged steeply enough to the yellow tide-wrack of Loch Beag.

But again and again my gaze was forced back to Eas-Coul-Aulin. There was no escape from the spell of the great fall, only endless fascination in watching the long thin spurts of white spilling and spinning down the cliff.

How should a waterfall be measured? This was a question that had been troubling me for some time without the consolation of any satisfactory answer. Should one, for example, wait until rain had caused a particularly heavy spate, or should the river in question be allowed no more than an average flow of water? Should a fall's rating depend on its longest single drop, or should overall height play a part in the assessment too? And what of the setting, what of the scale and magnificence of the surrounding rock scenery?

I examined Eas-Coul-Aulin more critically. The initial drop, although in wildly turbulent flood, was relatively short, measuring perhaps a mere 15 or 20 feet. Then followed three truly splendid leaps, more or less equal in height and interrupted by two explosive white cauldrons. At the foot, where the angle of the cliff lessened to a roof-top tilt, the fall split into a delta of minor cataracts and rivulets. The crux was, of course, the central section, and I tried to be as fair in my assessment as I could. In the end, I decided that each of the three plunges must measure approximately 150 feet, an estimate which agreed with the contour lines of the map and also with the known aneroid figure of 500 feet for the whole fall. This

Endrick journey.
Dr. Currie Henderson and the dinghy

meant that in ordinary conditions Eas-Coul-Aulin could not be acclaimed as the waterfall with the highest single drop; only after quite exceptionally heavy rain was it conceivable that the two intruding cauldron ledges might be eliminated, thus allowing the water a free fall of 400 feet or more.

But, I asked myself, was comparison after all of such vital importance? Did it really matter so very much where precisely Eas-Coul-Aulin stood in the list of Scottish waterfalls? I looked up at it once again falling splendidly free down the face of the great cliff and I found myself thinking of the Falls of Measach and the black depths of Corrieshalloch; of Foyers and of Bruar, of the amphitheatre of the Eas Mor, in Skye; I thought of Mr. George Scott-Moncrieff's "wonderful fiercesome, bleak and stark place . . . a little river winding through a remote and lifeless valley and plunging with absolute abruptness over a ledge of rock into a cauldron three hundred and fifty feet below"—the magnificent Falls of Glomach. Surely each had its own individual contribution to make, no less and no greater than any of the others, to the whole splendid pattern of Scotland's scenery.

The sun had gone in once more while we were busy with lunch, and mist was beginning to feather round the sharp prow of the Stack. It was time, unfortunately, to be on the move again. Faced with the strenuous climb back, we were almost tempted to avoid the detour up the glen by making a direct assault on the cliffs; some of the gullies, with their luxurious matting of sub-arctic scrub birch, looked quite straightforward scrambles. In the end, however, discretion won and we took the easy way round. We were all agreeably surprised to find how quickly we made height towards the lip of the waterfall and it was not long before we were able to make out the cloud-curtain of spray drifting slowly down wind across the side of the hill. Higher still we could feel it on our faces like fine rain.

The blink of fine weather had completely vanished, seemingly now for good, and on the zigzags leading to the col we climbed to the edge of trailing mist. The solitude about us was almost tangible and fancy suggested that we were in fact crossing some high pass on the frontiers of Tibet. It would scarcely have surprised us if we had suddenly come on a cairn decorated with prayer-flags, or met a procession of yaks, complete with Mongolian drivers.

However, the only encounter we did have was farther on, near the end of the walk, while we were toiling warm and weary across the last stretch of moor to the car. It was a man and a girl who approached towards us, both remarkably lightly clad. Indeed, as the young lady's somewhat striking ensemble included a pair of blue leopard-skin tights, with dainty blue and white sandals to match, we concluded that this was no more than the start of a gentle stroll.

But apparently we were wrong.

"Have you been over to the waterfall?" we were asked rather surprisingly and, it seemed, as nonchalantly as if we had been across the street to buy an evening paper. "This is the path, isn't it?"

We agreed that that was so. We also did our best to indicate that the fall lay on the far side of the pass, some hundreds of feet below the crest, which was now hidden in a pall of mist. A pointed look at our watches suggested, we hoped, that the shades of night were beginning to fall.

"Oh, yes," we were told, "but it's only three miles away." And the glances directed at our climbing boots and windproofs made quite clear the folly of carrying around such impedimenta.

Like Mr. Boffin, we stood watching for a little, "with hadmiration amounting to haw" as the ensemble resumed progress over the cutting flints of the path and in due course disappeared into the hollow beside Loch na Gainmhich. Then we turned and tramped on to the car.

Half an hour later, after a leisurely change and picnic tea, we turned the glasses on the point that the pair should have reached well up the slopes beyond the lochan. But the path was deserted; there was no sign of them anywhere.

We just hoped there would still be some July daylight left by the time they reached Eas-Coul-Aulin.

8

The River*

There are situations in life where it is wisdom not to be wise.

Schiller

AT a certain point in the course of the Second World War it happened that I was detailed to give instruction in the use of the rubber dinghy.

Just how much concern this event caused the German High Command will probably never be known, but I think it would be fair to say that it occasioned me a good deal more. It was, after all, an army duty of some novelty and one for which I seemed but poorly fitted, having never even seen a dinghy at close quarters until a couple of days previously.

However, I need not have worried. My success as a demonstrator was assured from the very first moment. Watched by my class of earnest students, I stepped smartly into the dinghy off the sea-wall of St. Ives harbour and fell head first over the bow into 14 feet of water.

Fortunately this proved to be no more than a temporary lapse. It did nothing to stifle in its infancy an affection for dinghying which was to grow and flower as time went on. Quite early on I had the notion—and the more I thought about it the more certain I became—that an immense new field of enjoyment was waiting for anyone who took seriously to the art of peace-time dinghying. In Scotland especially there was clearly endless scope for enterprise, similar of course to that open to the canoeists, yet with characteristics essentially its own.

Those were the days before the rubber dinghy had become a commonplace part of holiday amusement, and even when, a

* Five years after the river trip described in this chapter, in December 1963, my companion Dr. J. Currie Henderson collapsed and died shortly after setting off for a day on Ben Cruachan. Currie's friends remember him as a man of wide interests and immense keenness, and it is hoped that this story of an escapade in which he participated with all his typical enthusiasm will recall many of the other enjoyable days to which he contributed so much.

dozen years after the war, I decided it was high time to get down to some genuinely practical planning, the sight of cars with dinghy-burdened roof-racks was still comparatively rare.

During the intervening years it had been pleasantly easy to let the imagination run riot with a vague assortment of pipe-dreams. Now these had been narrowed down to a single definite plan—a journey down one of the rivers in the vicinity of Glasgow, the River Endrick. Rising some 1,500 feet up in the Fintry Hills in Stirlingshire, the Endrick makes a leisurely loop then flows westwards, crooked as Harry Lauder's walking-stick, to Loch Lomond. How much of its 28-mile course would be navigable, even by a dinghy drawing no more than a few inches of water, would have to be found out by trial and error during the actual expedition. All that could be said with reasonable certainty beforehand was that there would be enough novelty in the journey to make the whole thing well worth while.

In all this highly enjoyable planning there were just two snags, both rather obvious: I had no one to do the other half of the paddling and I had no rubber dinghy.

Such friends as I did venture to talk to about the scheme all showed an oddly similar pattern in their reactions: first the quick startled look; then the indulgent smile, as upon a child, and soothing words of sympathy; finally the hasty and rather sheepish change of subject. If I went a stage further and suggested actually teaming up, the victim could only stare, stricken to silence like a hunted animal at bay. Instead of a gentle pleasure outing, I might have been proposing a second Kon-Tiki expedition, 4,000 miles across the Pacific.

In the end, of course, the virtue of my cause had its reward. One evening I outlined my ideas to Dr. Currie Henderson, an old friend and a fellow-member of the Scottish Mountaineering Club. I reckoned there might be just a chance that he would be interested, as I remembered some of his descriptions of life as a doctor in one of the less hospitable parts of Africa and hoped that the prospect of a rather comfortless journey might perhaps have a nostalgic appeal. Psychologically, the moment chosen for broaching the subject could hardly have been worse, as he happened to be suffering from violent toothache. In case this should look too like taking an unfair advantage, I suggested sleeping on the proposal at least. But Currie would have none of it. With characteristic enthusiasm he gave me his answer there and then. Within a matter of minutes we were getting down to details, the offending tooth gallantly ignored.

The second of the problems—the quest for a dinghy—was even more difficult to solve.

Despite a methodical search there seemed to be nothing on sale exactly suited to our requirements; the shops—in the unenlightened days to which I refer—had quite astonishingly little to offer. Then someone suggested putting the query to the editor of one of the yachting magazines, and the latter, most helpfully, directed me to Birkenhead, to a firm of air-sea equipment manufacturers. A few days later I had details before me of a new dinghy just about to be marketed: the 3Y Multi-purpose Inflatable Boat. This looked, in the illustration, exactly what I had been used to during the war and exactly what we were looking for now. Obviously it was the ideal end to the hunt.

There remained just one last obstacle and it, of course, was financial. It was hard to argue that a 3Y dinghy costing an approximate £40 topped the list of priorities in the immediate family budget. Indeed it was not altogether easy to prove that it should be there at all. My wife was quite unreasonable on that score; but she was also quite decided.

Having got so far, however, a falter now was unthinkable. There was only one thing to do. I wrote yet another letter to Birkenhead, suggesting this time that, as I was unable to afford a dinghy, it might be possible to give me one. The reply was not the curt refusal I expected—and deserved; on the contrary, it exceeded all my hopes. I might, if I liked, have the 3Y on loan for one month. A sporting spirit must surely have prevailed round that Birkenhead boardroom table.

Once we were sure that the dinghy really was coming, we awaited its arrival with growing impatience. At last the great moment came and it was deposited with full pomp and ceremony at our door—a massive parcel of thick wrappings, endless string and protruding paddle-shafts. At once the younger members of the family fell upon it and literally tore the parcel to pieces. Quickly the contents were spread out in disarray on the garden lawn—black hull, plywood thwarts and paddles, bellows inflator, even a tin of repair solution. On first acquaintance the 3Y certainly looked a solid, serviceable job.

The same evening my daughter Helen and I took it along to Bingham's Boating Pond, just off Glasgow's Great Western Road. We hoped that growing darkness and a chilly nor'easter would discourage the curious, but we had no such luck and we had to labour at our task of inflating the ungainly black carcase in the middle of an embarrassingly inquisitive crowd. In the end we managed to fill it sufficiently full and carry it with faltering steps to the slipway. Then we launched forth under the attentive scrutiny of all—with a success that not even the crowd's most vocal critic could have denied.

The days that followed were busy with preparations for the Endrick journey. Yet when all was finally ready and I lay unsleeping into the small hours of D-Day morning, I felt as full of misgivings as Falstaff about what lay ahead: "I would it were bed-time, Hal, and all well."

In order to avoid unnecessary and possibly unwelcome attention on the river, Currie and I had decided on an Alpine start. We left Glasgow, therefore, an hour before dawn, waved on our way by Currie's wife Jenny, who was to meet us at journey's end later in the day. Unfortunately there was no such encouragement from the weather. The preceding week had been one of frequent thunderstorms, and deluge after deluge of rain had flooded the city streets. Now, as we drove through Blanefield and Killearn, the night seemed to close in about us and fierce lance-shafts of rain stabbed the glare of the headlights thick and fast. The world on the other side of the car windows was as disagreeable and inhospitable as it could be, and I at least derived precious little pleasure from the prospect of emerging into it. However, by the time we had reached our chosen launching point at the Balfron bridge, the rain had slackened and the great overburdened clouds had thinned sufficiently to allow us a little help from a fragment of waning moon.

We tugged out the dinghy from the back of the car and quickly had the hand-pump snorting and wheezing at its work. As we knelt to the task, now fumbling in black shadow, now emerging into the light of the moon or the car, it was impossible not to feel that we were a couple of conspirators about to embark on some evil felony.

"Better not use the torch," I muttered to Currie, as he went prowling off towards the river on a tour of discovery. "We don't want to attract undue attention at this hour of the morning even if we haven't got a splash-net with us." And the promptness with which he complied suggested that he was thinking much the same thoughts as I was.

Slowly—almost painfully slowly—the darkness lessened. Our watches showed five o'clock and everything was ready—dinghy inflated, plywood seats tied in, spare kit laid out; now we were growing impatient. Then at last the grey of dawn was spreading. As the cocks started to crow, up the road in Boquhan village, we heaved the dinghy over the metal gate by the bridge and carried it under a canopy of dripping trees. A short bank dropped from our feet to the Endrick, hissing past in full spate.

In discussing the trip beforehand, we had repeatedly mentioned one possible major snag: that there might be too little water. Yet, strangely enough, we had never worried about the possibility of there being too much. Now there was not the least doubt about the conditions: the black torrent swirling by in the half-light showed only too well what the effects of the recent thunderstorms had been. The character of the river had changed out of all recognition. This was disturbing enough for me, but for Currie—without even the reassuring experience of Bingham's Pond—the future must have had less attraction still. Yet it did not seem to be causing him any undue concern; on the contrary, the grin I could just make out as I watched him scramble aboard, seemed a fair indication of just how much he was enjoying himself.

We let go for'ard and aft at 5.20 a.m. precisely. The journey had begun.

For perhaps 100 yards all went well. Quickly the current caught us and we sped effortlessly down stream, while the bordering trees, black silhouettes, dropped astern in rollicking succession.

Then suddenly we heard rapids. The hiss and bubble were unmistakable and, peering into the half-dark ahead, we made out the leap of white crests. In a moment the dinghy was caught and whipped forward irresistibly, faster and faster, with the speed of a cork in a mill-race. In the wild turmoil around us the water slammed explosively on upthrust rocks, the noise seemingly magnified in echoes from the banks. By rights we should have been holed and sunk in the first 10 yards, yet somehow we went careering through unscathed, sucked with a twitch and a shudder into the very centre of the current and swaying drunkenly from side to side like the top deck of one of the old Glasgow tramcars. We fought hard to keep control and managed in fact to prevent hopelessly violent spinning, but it was too mad a rush for comfort and the harsh scrape of rubber upon rock was audible alarmingly often. The deck was thin and we could not rely indefinitely on luck rather than judgment to keep it intact. We paddled to the bank and drew breath.

This had, of course, been a clear warning to treat 'white water' with respect, but we were slow to heed it. We thought we might risk another short stretch, travelling gingerly. But the knack of proper control still eluded us and we found ourselves stranded on a shelf of rock, awash in a race of foam. I waded back to the bank once more and, grasping what turned out to be a clump of nettles with one hand, pulled the dinghy after me with the other. A few moments later Currie joined me on a stance of sloping, slippery mud.

It was at this point that the rain came on again—a malicious thunder-plump to add a little more to the discomfort of the stuffy, steamy morning. We decided to make a reconnaissance. Wielding a paddle apiece, we set off through a dripping jungle of chest-high willow herb and wild rhubarb. Soon we were soaking from head to foot and near to imagining ourselves on a military operation deep in some Malayan swamp. Even the outlook we did have was depressing; there was no escape unless by a hopelessly long portage.

Clearly necessity would have to be the mother of a certain amount of invention. We returned aboard and carried on cautiously downstream, but whenever really rough water showed up ahead, we paddled to the bank, disembarked and floated the dinghy past the difficulties. Without our weight it rode easily over any but the ugliest rocks. This was the answer to the problem, tiresome though it seemed to be. Soon we acquired the knack of slick team-work and gradually, too, we gained confidence. We learned to spot where the worst traps were hidden and even our paddling between whiles developed more obvious precision and purpose.

With the coming of full daylight our troubles seemed to diminish. The rain had eased once more and we became a little less conscious of the squalor slopping round our feet. We entered on a relatively quiet stretch of the river, where we could give ourselves up to enjoying the sheer luxury of just drifting. The only sounds to break the silence were, now and again, the scattering of twigs and leaves as some wood-pigeon or magpie made a startled getaway. Over the trees crowding thickly down to the left bank thin mist was lying like smoke from a camp fire and I had the momentary illusion that we had penetrated some remote corner of the Canadian backwoods. On the other side stretched a wide expanse of fields, where cows lifted their heads to look at us in amazement, for all the world as though they had never seen a rubber dinghy in their lives before.

These were the first moments of dawning contentment. As Currie remarked between tentative draws at his pipe: "This sort of dinghying certainly begins to make you feel that the whole thing might be worth while after all."

According to previous calculations, the first 2-mile 'leg' of the trip would take us to Drumtian Ford, down from Killearn village. Unfortunately, when eventually we arrived there, we had fallen a good deal behind schedule. Instead of the 2 miles per hour we had hoped for, our painstaking creep downstream had averaged just over one. This was not unduly worrying, with the whole day before us, but we soon discovered that instead of being able to make up any of the lost time, we were likely to lose more. The river became, if anything, more broken and a good many of the upthrust boulders showed rough textures which could have ripped holes in the dinghy's deck as easily as the teeth of a basking shark. Another hazard, too, presented itself: a barbed wire fence slung right across the river underneath the Aberfoyle road bridge. Here we had to land on a spit of shingle and mud, unload the dinghy and hoist it over the fence as gingerly as if we had been handling an heirloom tea-set of Crown Derby. Beyond that, however, we had our reward, with a glorious run of smooth, deep water. Turning a right-angled bend, the river glided through a majestic rock-gorge, dark and sheer-walled, over-arched by the picturesque span of the railway bridge. Here was a stretch worth all the hardships that had gone before, and we lolled back to enjoy the leisurely drift on the glassy black flood-water. We were passing through the canyon gateway to the huge horseshoe sweep which leads at its far end to the Pot of Gartness.

The Pot of Gartness is probably the most interesting and best known feature of the whole River Endrick. The seething cauldron and the formidable falls which pour into it make a magnificent sight, especially during a heavy spate, and no one could justly claim to know the West of Scotland properly without having on occasion made the familiar pilgrimage to watch the salmon leap. It was not the sort of place for a rubber dinghy—unless indeed with a more intrepid crew than ours— and I had made one or two previous reconnaissances along the banks in order to be quite certain how close to the falls we could safely go. We had been quite unanimous in our decision to take no chances.

There were, however, almost equally formidable obstacles to welcome us to the start of the bend. On the left bank a hostile dog, "a tousie tyke, black, grim and large", came bounding down from a small hut, with a baying and a baring of fangs that would have filled the crustiest Tibetan mastiff with envy. Directly ahead a steep weir fell away in a maelstrom of jagged boulders and spouting foam, the river then disappearing under a road bridge towards a succession of still wilder rapids beyond. On the right the third choice offered itself—a portage directly down the main street of the little village of Gartness.

We went to the right. At least the street was free from dogs.

The good people of Gartness were too polite to comment, except for one follower of Cassandra who emerged in his pyjamas to warn us in no uncertain terms of doom in the Pot; they merely left their breakfasts to stand at their front doors and stare. However, all the children of the village tagged on to the tail of our procession and solemnly watched our re-launching below the rapids. Possibly they were more envious of our sodden sport than their elders had been.

The rain had come on again more spitefully just before our portage and now as we approached the Pot itself it increased to a good-going deluge. The surface of the water fairly hissed with the raindrops, the trees dripped in unison, and soon we began to feel that if we had not been acting as sponges, the whole interior of the dinghy would have been awash.

We beached and spilled out what seemed like several gallons of water from its depths. Then we re-stowed the gear and began the further long spell of avoiding action round the Pot and its whirligig of rapids. We kept as close as we could to the bank, following a thread of a path, the thunder of the falls growing steadily louder as we skirted the rock-shelves where the eddies spun and tumbled. Then, abruptly, we were brought to a halt. To our amazement we found ourselves at the edge of a lawn, facing across to a well-tended rock-garden. Hastily we looked for a way round, but with no success at all; further progress could only be made directly opposite the front windows of the house.

"Well, here we are," I muttered to Currie, "I wonder if this is going to be journey's end."

All along throughout our planning we had speculated as to how officials and private individuals would react to our jaunt. Fishing rights, we knew only too well, were jealously preserved and our intrusion might quite justifiably be resented.

We had imagined ourselves under arrest, packed off to gaol, headlined in the Sunday papers. Facetious notions, of course, but containing enough sense in them to merit some heed. As citizens of nearly normal respectability we had found little pleasure in such a macabre prospect and we had even discussed the advisability of applying for permission, or indeed of switching to another river altogether. In the end, however, we had decided that these were no better than the symptoms of cold feet. There was nothing for it but to press on, pleading ignorance if necessary, and hoping for the best. Now, in contact again with civilisation, we seemed to have come to the showdown and it had no great attraction. There was obviously only one sensible way of crossing that lawn: to ask permission first. We advanced to the door and knocked.

What happened afterwards was scarcely what we had expected. Instead of reaching for his shotgun or the telephone, the owner of the house gave most cheerful permission. He even donned mackintosh and gumboots in order to come with us, in the teeming rain, and point out the best path to follow. We were relieved and mightily encouraged, and when we were actually helped with the dinghy over fences, through gates and down banks, our gratitude knew no bounds. With so much willing co-operation the detour became a pleasant interlude instead of, at the least, a costly waste of time. And, incidentally, we were intrigued to learn that just the year before a youth in a kayak had shot the falls and rapids of the Pot and lived to tell the tale. By comparison our own timid portage well out of range of anything even mildly dangerous seemed to make a thoroughly disappointing saga.

Once on our own again we scouted along the bank for the best place to re-embark, then relaxed for a little over a bar of chocolate. Another lull in the rain revealed encouraging tatters of blue sky, and when Currie fished out his pipe from the damp recesses of his windproof and proceeded to light up with more obvious success than previously, I sensed that our fortunes really were on the mend. And so in due course it proved: the next section of the journey, between 3 and 4 miles to the road bridge at Drymen, was afterwards declared to have been the most enjoyable of all.

We cleared the last genuine hazards almost at once: a patch or two of 'white water' and another barbed wire fence, treacherously low slung. Then the Blane Water came in on our left to bowl us along still more merrily on our way. From then on it was dinghying at its very best. We could see the traffic on the roads, yet we might have been 1,000 miles from its hustle and smell. We were travelling at an honest 2 knots, yet we scarcely needed to dip a paddle, even to check a spin, for it mattered not a whit which way we were facing, forwards, backwards, or sideways. The sun came out with a warmth that let us relax and bask like a couple of cats. And all the while the river uncoiled, bend after bend, with unlimited surprises: parties of mallard, crashing and splashing in agitated take-off; grey-green willows drooping exotic screens behind the great white arms of dead tree-trunks, half submerged; again a span of railway bridge, arched this time against genuine blue sky; fine country houses whose existence we had never even suspected;

and finally the fishermen, cheery youths greeting us from the banks and the shingle, united in a common bond of non-success.

We quickened our pace as we neared the 'milestone' of the Drymen road bridge, our paddles seeming to dip and rise with the rhythm of a Leander eight. A flock of some thirty green-shank scattered at our approach, banking steeply as they circled away with their nervous flickering flight. We watched them with pleasure while we turned in to a landing-place, recalling the wilder country of Sutherland where both of us had last seen birds of this kind.

It was now past midday, the hour set for our rendezvous at Loch Lomond. This meant that we had been falling steadily behind schedule all the way along and—much more serious— that Jenny Henderson would already be waiting for us near Balmaha. Her part in the day's programme was to collect us, bag and baggage, and take us back by car to our original launching point. Currie set off, therefore, for a nearby A.A. box to put through a pre-arranged message by telephone and also to inform my family that we were still afloat.

In the meantime I climbed up on to the sandy bank and fished out some rather overdue breakfast from the watery maw of my rucksack. At my feet lay the dinghy, and for a few minutes I let my thoughts centre on the grand service it had given us. It had stood up without protest to the harsh battering of the rapids; it had been dragged over stones and shingle and turf with no trace of a tear; it had been manhandled intact over jungles of thistles, barbed wire and jagged tree-stumps. If it now lacked a little air and felt rather like a soggy dumpling, that was scarcely surprising, since we had done no additional pumping in the seven hours of the trip. Indeed, we had every reason for gratitude that everything thus far had gone so well.

We had, of course, been lucky too. The fierce spate which had seemed so hostile in the chill half-light of dawn had, in fact, been our ally; under normal conditions the upper reaches of the river would undoubtedly have been too shallow for smooth progress. On the other hand, without such a violent current to nag and harry the dinghy downstream they might have been pleasant enough. It would be interesting to go back some lazy summer's day and put that idea to the test.

Ahead of us, between the Drymen bridge and journey's end at Loch Lomond wound 6 further miles. They looked on the map even more like a corkscrew than what had gone before, but we knew them to be comparatively harmless and agreed that only sheer bad luck could stop us now. The last actual obstacle of the day was the weir which spans the river underneath the Drymen bridge. Full of much sound and fury, the water here froths down a steep and jagged staircase, allowing little latitude for any but a dinghy crew of the wildest optimism. A glint in Currie's eye certainly betrayed how much he wanted to try conclusions with it, but in the end we voted against any heroics and instead portaged mildly to safety. When finally we did push off, from a stance of waterlogged turf, the tail-race of the fall set us spinning jauntily on our way and we tried to prolong its help as far as we could. Unfortunately the impetus lessened quickly and we began to notice also that even the main current was becoming more and more gentle. It was all too obvious that there could be no further leisurely drifting; a long afternoon of arduous paddling lay ahead.

The river itself ran into an extraordinary series of loops and kinks, majestic sweeps between overhanging banks of gay red sand. Some of the horseshoes bent so far round that, with a very little engineering, they might have been channelled into complete circles. The results at times were bewildering and decidedly tedious. For example, there was no escape from Buchanan Castle. Again and again we approached it and left it thankfully behind; again and again it appeared directly ahead in exactly the same position as before. Nor were we helped by the discomfort of our plywood seats. All day, hour after hour, we had fidgeted our way along on them, shifting position endlessly with little noticeable respite. At last Currie tried out an experimental shock-absorber by using one of our kapok life-jackets lying neglected and sodden in the slopping bilge-water. For the next few minutes we could do nothing but sit back in blissful relief.

Meanwhile the afternoon was passing with disconcerting speed. And on and on wandered the Endrick. Interminably it swung and wound between its jungle banks, where giant hemlock towered over close-serried ranks of iris sword-blades, occasional clumps of bulrushes and trailing yellow mimulus.

Beneath the black hull of the dinghy the blacker water mirrored the clouds, the current now completely sluggish and unhelpful. At times it seemed more fitting to imagine oneself out of Scotland altogether, on the Cherwell maybe, setting out for some leisurely punting in the warm gloaming of a June evening.

Round almost every corner we still kept surprising small parties of mallard; at the first glimpse of us they would be up and away in exciting disorder, banking over the trees with their swift, strong wing-beats. Less frequently we caught sight of moorhens, equally timid but choosing to scutter to safety in dark recesses of brushwood at the river's edge. Herons, too, were to be seen remarkably often and once, from a promontory of trees, a whole quintet of them flapped lazily away one after the other.

A slight breeze had got up soon after our last encounter with the castle and we found paddling into it unexpectedly irksome. The result was that we fell for the temptation of a good landing-place on a sandy spit and stopped for a little to stretch our legs. We also took another look at the map. Unfortunately, however, we failed to look at it closely enough and in consequence were in for a disappointment soon after our re-start. The Endrick finishes its course to the loch in an almost straight stretch of a mile and a half, and we imagined that we were just about to embark on that. Conic Hill, behind Balmaha, looked quite near, and we enjoyed watching the passing parade of shadows on its swelling brown slopes. Then ominously we swung away in yet another bend. First south-west, then south, then south-east we turned, until we were paddling in exactly the opposite direction. Instead of Conic Hill we faced Duncryne, the familiar pyramid hillock which overtops Gartocharn.

By this time we were beginning to feel really tired. The monotonous paddle-strokes, seemingly without end or respite, drew burning protests from muscles completely strange to the work. Like a couple of lotus-eaters, we thought with longing of the earlier luxury of drifting downstream with the current:

> ... but evermore
> Most weary seem'd the sea, weary the oar,
> Weary the wandering fields of barren foam.

Then, almost suddenly, we were round the last bend. And

A bend of the River Endrick, near Drymen

this time, unmistakably, it was the final straight that stretched before us. There once again was Conic Hill and, more nearly dead ahead, the treetops of Inchcailleach, shaped like the top-knot of an Indian brave. Our morale gave a joyous upward surge and our paddles dipped in unison with a fresh spurt of energy.

We had turned once more into the face of the frisky bit of breeze, blowing now directly across the loch and in at the mouth of the river. It ruffled the water into a miniature ploughed field, so that the dinghy went bouncing and bumping rather ludicrously from wavelet to wavelet. It also gave us some more hard work, but we cared little for that now and drove forward eagerly. In front of us the horizon had expanded to a great sweep of hills, while behind stretched a glorious Constable landscape, green and silver foreground, brown Duncryne, and over all in the blue afternoon sky, bright islands of cloud. Gradually the mouth of the river widened and merged into the wind-rippled grey of the loch.

There was nothing dramatic about the end of the journey. Indeed, with extensive flooding all round, it was impossible to define the exact pattern of river bank and loch shore. But as we paddled indecisively in on the last few yards, carefully avoiding the skeletons of innumerable dead trees, precise details mattered little. Our contentment was complete.

"Finished with engines," grunted Currie, as he shipped his paddle for the last time. "Twelve hours exactly since we pushed off."

"Feels like it too," I answered, climbing slowly and stiffly ashore. "And a bit of work yet, I'm afraid, till we reach the road."

But even the half-mile carry that really did end our labours was quickly accomplished and soon forgotten. For up by the roadside we made prompt contact with Jenny Henderson and Seonaid and Jimmy, our invaluable, long-suffering support party. What they might have said to describe their six-hour wait scarcely bore thinking about. But we were spared the reprimand we so justly deserved. Instead, we at once found ourselves enjoying the cheeriest of picnics, with soup and sandwiches and cake and coffee—a welcome as royal as it was unmerited.

At journey's end, Loch Laidon.
Lindley Carstairs, the hat and the dinghy

And so was added the final touch of warmth to the spreading glow of our satisfaction. We might even have added the summing up of Robert Louis Stevenson: "After a good woman, and a good book, and tobacco, there is nothing so agreeable on earth as a river."

9

The Moor

Rannoch Muir . . . that thorofare of thieves.
Breadalbane Papers

AFTER the trip down the Endrick there still remained three valuable weeks for further adventuring with the dinghy.

Various schemes suggested themselves, some practicable, others perhaps of less commendable wisdom. Each had its own special attractions, of course, and could certainly be said to offer the chance of seeing another bit of Scotland in a novel way; it was clear enough now that dinghying need never suffer from banality.

There was, however, one project which seemed to me to be outstanding, to occupy a position of pre-eminence above all the others—a dinghy crossing of the Moor of Rannoch.

On first consideration the merits of this idea are not perhaps particularly obvious; one thinks, after all, of Rannoch Moor as not much more than a vast expanse of heather, or as Dr. John Macculloch graphically put it, "an inconceivable solitude, a dreary and joyless land of bogs, a land of desolation and grey darkness". But a look at the map quickly shows the error of this belief. A magnificent waterway is seen to stretch right across the Moor from the Glencoe road, via Loch Ba, the Abhainn (River) Ba and Loch Laidon, all the way to Rannoch railway station on the old West Highland line. Even the most unimaginative would surely admit that this looks a dinghy route of the highest order and one thoroughly well worth following.

Doubtless by comparison with some of the West Coast exploits of the canoeists such a trip would be insignificant. Yet I felt nevertheless that it would have an interest of its own; that the outcome, linked to the Endrick experiment, might give the key to a variety of inland voyages of character. I thought, for instance, of that tremendous waterway in Sutherland reaching south-eastwards from Loch Laxford to Lairg, a

40-mile chain of loch and river. Or at the other end of the country there was the Nith awaiting exploration all the way from the high hinterland of Ayrshire to the Solway. Putting the clock back, I recalled the epic journey carried out by the late Rev. T. Ratcliffe Barnett and a friend as long ago as 1890, when they sailed and paddled their home-made *Kelpie* across central Scotland via the Clyde and Loch Lomond, Loch Katrine and Loch Achray, Loch Vennachar and the Forth, to Grangemouth, then back home to Paisley by canal. Our journey would be nothing to such a marathon as that, yet there was no saying how it might be extended and elaborated by anyone who had a mind to do so.

Undoubtedly the most remarkable crossing of the Moor of Rannoch ever to be made was accomplished at the very end of January 1889. The party consisted of seven men—three civil engineers, the head of a firm of contractors, two estate factors and a solicitor—and their ages ranged from 28 to 60. Only one had been across the moor before. The purpose of the journey was to obtain further information about the route which the projected West Highland Railway was to follow across the waste of peat hags and heather, of confusing ridges and black, sluggish streams. The most valuable item of equipment carried on this expedition venturing out in the depths of a Highland winter appears to have been an umbrella.

From the start everything went wrong. The direction of the crossing was to be from north to south, and the first day's programme was to travel from Spean Bridge to a remote shooting lodge at the southern end of Loch Treig. The weather was atrocious, the boat on the loch ancient and leaky, and when eventually they reached the lodge, towards midnight, it was to find that they were totally unexpected. Next morning, nevertheless, they pressed on: in driving sleet they climbed to the highest point of the moor at 1,300 feet and faced the track-less wilderness ahead. A meeting had been arranged beside the River Gaur with one of the local landowners, but this misfired and by the time they had decided to carry on to their destination, still 14 miles away, only some three hours of daylight were left. It was not long before they became separated; several were utterly exhausted. One tripped over a fence and lay stunned for four hours. When he came to, however, he realised that fences on the moor are few and far between and that this one must lead to some kind of a house. Following it in the darkness, he stumbled eventually on Gorton cottage. Shepherds were quickly out with lights and, guided by the shouting from various directions, helped the bedraggled travellers to the sanctuary of a small hut. A peat fire was made and gradually the party dried out. Next day they were taken by cart to Inveroran Inn, where they were made cheerily welcome. That night a severe blizzard broke over the whole of the West Highlands.

As dinghy-partner on this occasion—which I hoped would be rather less dramatic—I was delighted to have my cousin-in-law Lindley Carstairs, companion on so many previous mountain days from Ben Hope in Sutherland to The Merrick in Galloway and from Kintail to the Braes of Angus. This, of course, would be an expedition of a different kind altogether, and Lindley's action in volunteering for the unknown seemed to me to be especially commendable. We had hoped to have Currie Henderson with us also, in what would have been perhaps rather a cramped threesome, but much to his disappointment and ours he was unable to take time off for this second journey.

Lindley and I soon discovered that we had plenty of details to consider, for the plan of campaign was of necessity rather complicated. No road, as yet, runs across the moor, only the railway line, so that our return to base from our destination at Rannoch station would have to be by rail, with the dinghy duly deflated and stowed for carrying. The idea was therefore that we should leave Glasgow after work on Friday evening and drive in two cars to Bridge of Orchy station, which lies on the southern fringe of the moor some 15 miles south of Rannoch. There one of the cars would be left. We would then carry on together in the second car to the launching-point beside Loch Ba, which comes conveniently to within a hundred yards or so of the road. By that time it would be dark, but with some generous help from the moon we reckoned there should be little difficulty in travelling through the night. The point of doing the trip in this rather odd way was that there would be plenty of time to catch the Saturday morning train back from Rannoch to Bridge of Orchy, yet if things did go far wrong and we missed it, there would still be a comfortable margin before the afternoon train was due. There are no trains at all on Sunday and we had no wish to be stranded at Rannoch until Monday.

We eventually fixed on the Friday of the autumn holiday, the last week-end in September, when there would be a full moon. Our decision was the signal for the usual break-down in the weather. Each day of the preceding week seemed worse than the one before. Rain whipped the city streets and on some of the higher hills there was a peppering of the first snow-showers of the winter. On Wednesday the wind rose to a paroxysm of fury, while on Thursday even the weather forecast seemed as though it might be accurate for once: "High winds with gales in places and frequent heavy showers; thunder at times."

Then, on Friday, a sudden miraculous change set in. The wind dropped and the clouds dispersed. All day long the sun shone and in its warmth our faded optimism re-emerged and flourished anew. By the time Lindley and I were making our separate ways northwards in the evening the serenity of the sky gave a promise that looked unbreakable.

We met as arranged at Bridge of Orchy and in the gathering gloaming loaded all the gear into one car. As we moved off again, across the darkening moors and round the great curve and climb beyond Loch Tulla into sight of Loch Ba itself, we felt with a surge of elation that we were really under way at last.

As at the beginning of the Endrick trip, there seemed to be something rather furtive about drawing off the road and starting to pump air into the unwieldy carcase of the dinghy. Lindley had brought a large electric carriage lamp, and into and out of its beam we moved like a couple of poachers at work on a clandestine gralloch. Frequently we found ourselves caught in the headlight glare of passing cars and we felt guiltily conspicuous as we crouched and fumbled at our task. The pumping seemed endless and during my spells of toil I found myself counting the strokes by hundreds, after the time-honoured manner of a step-kicker on a monotonous mountain snow-slope. In addition the two inlet valves gave a certain amount of trouble and in the end we had to leave off pumping with the pressure rather less than we should have liked. We sealed the valves doubly tight with balloon rubber and corks, then, hoping for the best, hoisted the dinghy in triumph shoulder high and moved off on our 100-yard carry down to the edge of the loch.

The night was very quiet and almost windless. Above the hunched shoulder of Beinn Creachan the moon was just up. Momentarily it was withdrawn behind a veil of cloud, but this was fortunately not so dense as to cause any anxious qualms. Already the lanes of silver which its light projected across the moor made striking contrast with the black corners of the loch. Against the peat at our feet the water lay absolutely still, as dark and mysterious as the contents of Gaelic coffee. Gingerly we lowered the dinghy to the bank and let it slip into the water.

I think it must have been just about this time that I first happened to notice my companion's hat. Up till then I had been concentrating on all the various preparations for the launching, but suddenly, in a moment of awful revelation, I became aware of what surmounted Lindley's head. In shape one might have said that it resembled an inverted casserole, or possibly that type of shako worn by some regiments of foot during the Peninsular War. Even in the moonlight I could see that it was made of some kind of hairy material, akin perhaps to coconut matting.

"What on earth is that?" I gasped.

"What's what?" replied Lindley, no doubt sensing the trace of anxiety in my voice.

"The thing on your head. Is it a spare bailing can or something?"

Lindley drew himself up to his full height. "I've been waiting for months for a suitable occasion to put on this hat and I think this is it. I'd have imagined you'd be the first to agree."

"All right," I said, as soothingly as I could. "Wear the thing if you must, only I'd rather you occupied the rear seat in the dinghy if you don't mind."

We pushed off, hat and all, at 8.20 p.m. As we paddled gently, almost hesitantly, away, out of the inky black shadow of our inlet, there was a feeling of utter unreality about the whole venture. It was like the start of an operational sortie in wartime and one felt like talking in whispers, when in fact a shout would have gone unheard. The occasional squeaking of paddle-shafts meeting rubber seemed queerly out of keeping with the silence of the night.

The problem of Loch Ba, the first stage of our journey, was its extraordinarily complex maze of islands. They confronted us at once, some large, others mere boulder-reefs and shoals, round all of which it was hopelessly difficult to choose the right way to steer. The moonlight added to the deception, laying subtle traps in silver and black, while our eyes were still unused to measuring distances or gauging horizons. Several times we had to paddle back and choose a new avenue and once or twice we quite simply ran aground. Gradually, however, we made distance; now we could distinguish the familiar outline of Buachaille Etive Mor, blacker than the black sky, away over to the west; slowly but surely the car headlights on the road, ranging over the heather like lighthouse beams, fell farther and farther astern.

After half an hour or so we paused for a short rest and a bite of chocolate and fruit.. We had steered well out towards the middle of the loch and laid down our dripping paddles without regret. Round us the water had the look of black ice, hiding unfathomable depths. We scarcely spoke, listening for preference to the silence. Utter quiet lay about us, save once only when we heard the sounds of a train in the distance, somewhere over the moor near the old Wood of Crannach.

Such silence, such utter quiet, I reflected, was infinitely worth a quest like this. What greater contrast could we have found to the daily round, to the time-menaced scurry of the city, than this brief rest on an Argyllshire lochan, motionless under the stars? It was good to pause for a little and consider; to have a glimpse, even if only for a minute or two, of the sort of things we miss in our endless preoccupation with the everyday urgencies, which, for all our hustling, never seem to grow less.

Our troubles with the islands were not yet at an end and soon after our re-start we found ourselves involved once more. An avenue of silver, bright in the moonlight, looked as though it should be the way ahead, only to mock us like a will o' the wisp at the last moment by turning out to be an isthmus of sand. We made a sharp hairpin bend back to port only to find big boulders guarding another jutting point. Inevitably we cut the corner too fine and there was a harsh grating noise as the belly of the dinghy caterpillared over rough rock.

"Just as well it's made in two compartments," I remarked, as we pushed off again and steered out into a deeper channel. "If one half gets punctured the other is guaranteed to keep us afloat."

"That's a comfort," replied Lindley. "I suppose I'd better take your word for it. Only, if I remember aright, that's what they said about the *Titanic*."

Happily the argument was never put to the test. We paddled on with optimism undimmed.

For some time now we had been looking ahead to the hill-slopes silhouetted against the eastern sky. Almost suddenly they seemed to be very much nearer. If, as now looked decidedly likely, they actually ran down to the moor between Loch Ba and Loch Laidon, then we must be very nearly at the end of the first stage of the journey. Such good progress would have been too good to be true by previous Endrick standards, but this time there had been no interruptions and the pace in consequence had been much steadier. Our hopes certainly rose, and when the channel ahead narrowed to canal width, between banks fringed with moor grass, our paddle-strokes quickened expectantly.

Then unmistakably we heard the sound of a river. Here would be proof positive: if it were flowing *out* of the loch, it could only be the Abhainn Ba, the middle link in our chain. We nosed the dinghy against the bank and walked forward to prospect. Then, to avoid deception in the moonlight, we bent down and peered intently at the current. Yes, indeed, it was flowing east. Loch Ba was behind us and we were well ahead of schedule.

This was our point of no return. Once past here it would become progressively easier to carry on to Rannoch station, more difficult to work our way back to the Glencoe road. So we had decided in our planning beforehand. For, of course, we had always had to reckon with the possibility of unforeseen misfortune, such as hopelessly hostile weather, or some mishap to the dinghy.

I put it to Lindley—knowing perfectly well what he would answer—that he might like to go back.

"No, indeed," he said, looking round for a good place to hoist the dinghy from the water. "That would be a poor idea. Let's see a bit more of Rannoch Moor."

I just hoped that what we did see of it during the next few hours would not be more than enough.

Between Loch Ba and Loch Laidon lies a stretch of moorland about a mile wide. Across this winds the connecting river, the Abhainn Ba, trending first south-eastwards, then slightly north of east. The difference in altitude between the two lochs is about 100 feet, so our hopes of being able to dinghy down were not at all high. What we saw merely confirmed our expectations. The Abhainn Ba was an honest Highland burn, some 15 yards wide, tumbling tunefully along through a maze of spray-flecked boulders. Its channel looked, in the moonlight, as unwelcoming as the wildest of the 'white water' on the Endrick. There were no two ways about it: the moor ahead would need a long and exacting portage.

We re-stowed the gear in the damp depths of the dinghy and shoved in the paddles on top, then, taking an end each, we set off over the heather.

The sky had been scoured clear of the last shreds of cloud and the moon was riding free. Round us its light spilled in profusion over a sea of hummocks and hollows, the yellow autumn colours of the moor grass suggesting the sands of some limitless Sahara. At first the going was easy, over heather that was short, springy and obligingly level. Then it began to deteriorate. Ditch-sized burns kept crossing our path and every now and again the moonlight deceived us into stepping confidently on to the green moss of bogs. As we went squelching ankle-deep into the icy water, our gym-shoes, damp before, became completely sodden and cold. Then the angles tilted and the ground became rougher. We met stiffer rises and, in between, deeper hollows, always set across our line of advance. Most of the latter contained peat-hags with steep or overhanging edges, and through them we slipped and slithered in erratic discomfort. I could not help thinking once again of Dr. Macculloch's description, written apparently with some feeling nearly a century and a half ago:

Pray imagine the moor of Rannoch; for who can describe it.

A great level (I hope the word will pardon this abuse of it) 1,000 feet above the sea, sixteen or twenty miles long, and nearly as much wide, bounded by mountains so distant as scarcely to form an apprehensible boundary; open, silent, solitary; an ocean of blackness and bogs, a world before chaos; not so good as chaos, since its elements are only rocks and bogs, with a few pools of water, bogs of the Styx and waters of Cocytus, with one great, long, sinuous, flat, dreary, black Acheron-like, lake, Loch Lydog, near which arose three fir trees, just enough to remind me of the vacuity of all the rest. Not a sheep nor a cow; even the crow shunned it, and wheeled his croaking flight far off to better regions. If there was a blade of grass any where, it was concealed by the dark stems of the black, black, muddy sedges, and by the yellow, melancholy rush of the bogs.

Under any circumstances crossing such country on foot is apt to be tiresome; when one is anchored inescapably to the end of a rubber dinghy, even less can be said in its favour. We tried changing hands and we tried changing ends; we tried hoisting the thing on to our shoulders, on to our backs, even on to our heads—all to no avail. There was no easy answer; we were shackled to our boat as inexorably as any pair of galley-slaves to their oar. And so there was nothing for it but to put up with it all, while muscles ached and throbbed and finally burned white hot in protest, with the torments of Burns's toothache:

> An' thro' my lug gies mony a twang,
> Wi' gnawing vengeance,
> Tearing my nerves wi' bitter pang,
> Like racking engines!

And then, quite suddenly, Loch Laidon was below us. Weary and out of breath, we topped a heather rise and there it lay, a narrow sheet of quicksilver reaching away into the dim background of the night. Thankfully we covered the last couple of hundred yards to its edge and shed our burden on a broad, grassy bank.

There we had our reward. We picnicked at the outflow of the Abhainn Ba, just below its last rollicking gallop over the boulders. The moon was at its brightest, high overhead, so that we could see every detail of the burn as it came racing downhill towards us in a torrent of tossing white foam. The night was still calm and pleasantly mild and so bright that we might almost have been sitting down to our morning elevenses, had the time been precisely twelve hours different. It was a relief after the encounter with the peat-hags to lean back and relax, and when Lindley produced a flask of coffee to go with our sandwiches, our comfort seemed complete.

For a little while my fancy drifted idly away, to lose itself somewhere far down Loch Laidon, where dark water merged into dark sky. Everything seemed utterly unreal in this world of moonlight and silence. It was not very difficult to think of it as having the kind of atmosphere in which some of the old-time Highland legends were born, legends maybe of such supernatural beings as the *each uisge*, the much-dreaded water-horse, or the half human, half fairy *glastig*. Was there, I wondered, a water-horse ranging the shores of Loch Laidon, with peculiarities like those of its forerunner of Loch Avon, in the Cairngorms? It would be quite a triumph to arrive at Rannoch with one in tow behind the dinghy, although according to the old tales the only hope of taming one was to make use of a silver bridle, the alternative being to be carried off to a watery grave in the loch.

I took rather a furtive glance at Lindley out of the corner of an eye. He seemed, however, to be having a more prosaic session with a bacon and egg roll, gazing in perfect contentment at the burn. There was no apparent evidence that in thought he was locked in mortal strife with a *glastig*.

After half an hour we bestirred ourselves once more. It would have been extremely pleasant to stay and bivouac where we were, but we had agreed that it would be advisable to put as many as possible of Loch Laidon's 5 miles behind us during the night rather than wait until morning. Anything might happen to hold us up and we had no wish to finish the journey in a flurry of haste to catch the train. We therefore gathered together our gear, stowed it in a pile like the old clothes counter at a jumble sale, and launched away. Soon the song of the Abhainn Ba had begun to grow faint behind us.

Loch Laidon is comparatively narrow, and deep in places, so we decided that it would be wise to keep within reasonable swimming distance of the shore. We chose the eastern side and soon were paddling along, close in, to a steady harmonious rhythm. The exercise kept us warm—except for our feet, which felt wet and cold beyond hope of recovery—and in addition we had the satisfaction of knowing that every hundred yards we 'stole' in this way represented another slice off the long stretch ahead of us in the morning.

That first hour of Loch Laidon was, for me at least, the most enjoyable of the whole expedition. For it alone, all our planning and all our toil would have been infinitely worth while.

There was still not a breath of wind to ruffle the mirror-surface of the water and, with time mattering nothing, we slipped along almost without conscious effort. We rounded jutting promontories and passed bay after shingle bay backed by the silhouettes of heather banks. Scarcely a word was exchanged, for we were once again in a world of silence, silence so complete that we felt inclined to dip our paddles with stealth, as though to do otherwise would have been sacrilege. The moon was behind us and our own black shadows cut strange-shaped notches in the track of silver ahead. And above us blazed the stars in brilliant profusion, arching through the stupendous span of Plough and Pole Star to where Capella hung like an emperor's diamond near the scintillating crown of the Pleiades.

It was one of those nights which possess that quality of beauty so far beyond the power of words to describe, which turn back the pages of memory to other, comparable experiences by moonlight—an open tent door black-rimming the floodlit splendour of Glen Etive; the saw-edge of the Cuillin above frosted moors, the spires of Sgurr Alasdair and Sgurr Sgumain jet against the dancing white of the aurora; the ridge of Cruachan, its crest of corniced snow a delectable switchback, crisp, glittering, inviting. . . .

But our idyllic spell of paddling had to come to an end some-time. Inevitably our arm muscles began to tire and as our strokes became more laborious, so gradually they lost rhythm—and pleasure. In addition a night breeze was at last springing up, blowing into our faces from across the bleak miles of the moor. Admittedly it was still gentle enough, but for all that it quickly furrowed the loch and despite all our protective cloth-ing struck an icy chill. By 1 a.m. it had become obvious that it was high time for us to go ashore and bed down for what remained of the night.

It was not until we had shipped our paddles and stumbled unsteadily from the slopping puddle inside the dinghy that we realised how desperately cold we had become. Our legs almost creaked as we tried to straighten them, and our feet, now quite without feeling, seemed separated from us in a squelching, skidding world of their own. The landing-place we had chosen turned out to be much less sheltered than we had expected, for the ground immediately behind it was no better than a shallow scoop, floored with large angular boulders and scraggy heather that put one in mind of some corrie in the Cairngorms. In the midst of this paradise we tottered about, our teeth chittering, in the woolly hope that we might find a few level square feet on which to spread out our sleeping-bags.

Then, just at exactly the right moment, Lindley came to the rescue. From a hidden corner at the bottom of his rucksack he fetched out some Bovril and yet another flask, this time containing hot water. A few seconds later I had a steaming cup in my hand and could feel the comforting warmth literally flowing through me. That nightcap made all the difference just when it was most urgently needed.

The only drawback, I found, was that the glow did not extend to my feet. Even when I was able to thrust them far down into the depths of my sleeping-bag, they felt miserably like refrigerated lead. Nor was there much chance to improve matters at all by wriggling about; the ground underneath was so like a mountain scree-slope that the only way to stretch out was to insinuate oneself into a kind of narrow slalom course of boulders, in which a jerk one way bumped the right knee and a turn the other grazed the left elbow. I tried to console myself with Gino Watkins's dictum born on the Greenland ice-cap that "mere cold is a friend, not an enemy", but the remedy had no marked success.

For compensation there was an outlook from our bivouac-site of truly memorable beauty. We had fetched up directly opposite Eilean Iubhair, the 'yew tree island', and in the brilliant moonlight its outline lent variety to the silver of Loch Laidon and the dark contours of the moor. Loch Ba and the Abhainn Ba seemed very far away now, lost in obscurity beyond the bays and promontories we had just passed, but in silhouette 10 miles off, Buachaille Etive Mor made a symmetrical background with the slightly nearer bulk of Meall a' Bhuiridh, across the notch of Glen Etive.

It was behind these hills, about 6 a.m., that we watched the moon go down. Till the last segment vanished, its light competed with the early sun and it was impossible not to feel grateful for the bountiful service it had given us all through the night. If it had failed us and bad weather had supervened, our journey would almost certainly have had to be abandoned.

We got up without enthusiasm. We were feeling stiff and chilled, and we could not help turning a rather hostile eye on the dinghy, slumped sloppily by the edge of the loch in its dry dock of boulders. For the moment at least it had become the author of all our discomfort. Boating on remote Highland lochs seemed a sport of singularly little charm.

However, after some sandwiches and chocolate, our morale improved slightly and we even summoned up sufficient energy to pump a little air into the dinghy. It seemed particularly slow to respond and when we pushed off, just before seven o'clock, it still felt more like a suet pudding than we might have wished.

It was a lovely morning with a true autumn hint of frosts in store. The sun was slow to reach us, skulking behind thin cloud even after it was fully up. We watched it impatiently as we plied our dripping paddles and looked with envy at the western hillside which was already warmly patterned. What mist there was lay right down on the loch, rising gently from the water like steam. Its eddies filled the bays and blurred the outline of the shore, leaving only a few thin banks trailing farther out. Now and again we could hear stags roaring and over the moor we watched small herds of deer on the move. Grouse were about in plenty too, taking wing from the heather with harsh scolding. One old fellow, perched cockily on a tussock, made an unusual landmark for us as we worked our way quietly past.

After a short time we began to notice a rather sinister hissing sound which seemed to be issuing from one at least of the dinghy's inlet valves. Neither of us liked to mention this at first and we went paddling on stolidly, doing our best to make believe that we were concentrating on the scenery. It was a little disconcerting all the same just to sit waiting and listening, wondering the while if one final outrush of air would sink us like a stone in a grand gurgle of bubbles. In fact, it seemed rather foolish. So in the end we gave way and switched course, nose to shore, beaching finally on a small rocky headland. The trouble turned out to be what we had suspected and it took us no more than a few minutes to put it right, with a little honest pumping and some manipulation of our cork and rubber bungs. This was the one and only defect encountered in the dinghy on either of its two major trips; otherwise our confidence in it was complete.

Meanwhile, just to plague us, a breeze had begun to blow up the loch. There was little strength in it and certainly no malice, but we were glad all the same to have put Loch Laidon's first miles so well and truly behind us. The pause on the headland to mend the valves had been a welcome break in the monotony, but now as the water wrinkled ahead of us, our paddles felt suddenly heavier and our pace grew slower; solitary trees on the loch-side, by which we could measure our onward creep, took aeons of time to approach and pass and fall astern; instead of being thoroughly grateful for the sunlight now flooding about us, we took its joyful warmth for granted. Without a doubt we were beginning to look forward to taking life easy again.

Then, at last, we were able to make out familiar details beyond the head of the loch: the dark smudge of Rannoch station and close beside it the more prominent landmark of the long railway viaduct. As we looked, the smoke of a train mushroomed upwards and drifted slowly down wind. Instinctively we glanced at our watches. But there was no need for panic. This was only the early train northbound from Glasgow to Fort William; there was still plenty of time before ours, heading south, was due.

As we started on the loch's last mile, our spirits rose again. Straight ahead was our final objective, the sickle of golden beach that stood for the end of all our striving and toil; with mounting excitement we watched it drawing steadily nearer.

On our right a long headland, topped with a single pine tree, reached out towards the middle of the loch and we surmised that in the recess beyond it lay concealed the outflow of the River Gaur. With more time to spare we should have

Backward view down the length of Loch Laidon

liked to fit in a morning's reconnaissance, exploring this corner where the river has its birth and starts on its lively descent towards Bridge of Gaur. If only it were navigable, what a superb link it would make in the obvious sequel to our Rannoch crossing! Down to Loch Rannoch itself, then on to the challenge of Tummel and Tay; some day it might be that we would return and try out possibilities for ourselves.

We altered course slightly to port, paddling close in under the heather-crowned banks of the northern shore and aiming eventually for the nearest corner of the beach. Up on the slopes above we could pick out the kinks and switchbacks of the track which runs parallel to the water's edge and which clearly makes pleasant going hereabouts. Two hikers off the morning train, weighed down by enormous rucksacks and heading westwards for the moor, were making their way along it. As they came level with us they gave us a wave and a cheery shout.

A hundred yards—50—20—10—steadily the gap narrowed. Then quite suddenly the dinghy was crunching on small shingle, gently-angled. It slid to a stop and we sat back, laying aside our dripping paddles. I turned to face Lindley, smiling broadly beneath the expansive brim of the shako. Then I shook him by the hand; it was, I reckoned, a suitably solemn occasion.

After a little we stood up and stepped ashore, tugging at the dinghy till it was high and dry beside us on the beach. And so, quietly and undramatically as on the Endrick, the journey ended. Everything had gone according to plan. Our luck with the weather had been perfect; the dinghy had maintained its high standard of reliability; the last miles of Loch Laidon had not, after all, turned into a wild race against the clock. As my thoughts went jerkily over the rather odd sequence of events from the idea's birth to the actuality of our final exhilarating touch-down, my satisfaction could not have been more complete.

We deflated the dinghy and stuffed it unceremoniously into its canvas container along with the rest of our gear. Then, with the whole thing suspended from the paddles, we laid these on our shoulders and set off, like a couple of Chinese coolies, along the path to Rannoch station.

Autumn reflections. A corner of Loch Katrine

Behind us Loch Laidon was mirror calm, for the breeze had fallen away again. Even so it was not too difficult to imagine the tribulation we might have had to endure, had the weather kicked up really rough. The track we were now treading so peacefully might well have seemed a very long way indeed.

We reached the station in good order and soon were in the throes of sorting out the bewildering muddle of our kit. This done, we tackled the more serious business of second breakfast and even managed to take some thought to our appearances. Then the train came clanking in and we hoisted ourselves and the gear aboard into an unpopular huddle in the corridor.

Barely an hour later we were back at our old 'advanced base' close beside Loch Ba.

The return journey had been accomplished absurdly quickly. Indeed it had been almost depressing to watch from the train windows how the miles of the moor slipped past. Loch Laidon a brief last glint of silver; the brown slopes of Beinn Creachan; the pines of the old Wood of Crannach; Achaladair farm; the familiar surroundings of Loch Tulla—one picture had followed the other in close sequence, like the spinning of a well-known film in reverse. Maybe, having sampled these few minutes of superficial viewing, we could value the more what we had gained from our own painstaking creep to the east.

Now, as we stood at the roadside beside the parked cars, we let time slow down once again. It was a lovely September morning. Over the patchwork browns and yellows of Rannoch Moor the sun streamed free, while up on Stob Ghabhar the long ridges seemed to crown with a halo of light the dark recesses of the corries.

We strolled over towards the edge of the loch and gazed idly across its quiet blue water. Automatically our thoughts went back over the events of the past sixteen hours, the experiences we had had since first we started puzzling out our island-dodging in the moonlight. Now the adventure was over. There was nothing more to it except the prosaic drive back to the city.

But as I turned to the final task of loading up the cars I realised that whatever sailing I might happen to do in days to come, I would always think with especial gratitude of the dinghy and the two trips it had made possible. As the Tar remarked of the *Vital Spark*: "I've seen a wheen o' vessels since I left her, but none that had her style nor nicer shupmates."

The Glen

And thus an airy point he won,
Where, gleaming with the setting sun,
One burnish'd sheet of living gold,
Loch Katrine lay beneath him roll'd.

Sir Walter Scott

FOR long enough it had seemed quite wrong that there should be, almost on our doorstep as it were, a glen with a history and one which I had literally never set eyes on, and a loch, one of the most celebrated in Scotland, which I had seen occasionally from afar but never rightly visited. Yet there was Rob Roy's Glen Gyle, only just over the boundary in the next county to ours and virtually clamouring for a first encounter; and there next to it was Loch Katrine, immortalised by Sir Walter Scott, stretching back invitingly from the Trossachs a mere hour's car-run from home.

Clearly glen and loch could be combined in the best possible kind of visit—in a walk to be vastly enjoyed at the time and long remembered afterwards. Starting-point would be at the foot of Glen Falloch, at Beinn Ghlas farm; the finish obviously at the Trossachs. The more closely it was studied on the map, the more attractive-looking did the expedition become.

Surprisingly, there was no difficulty about finding a companion for the proposed $13\frac{1}{4}$-mile marathon. My wife Mais in particular was keen to come, eager for the chance to renew an acquaintance with Loch Katrine which was considerably better than mine; unfortunately, however, she had to decide to put other duties first. In the end I was delighted to have Norman Easton as the other half of the party. Norman and I had been together on more Scottish 'Munros' than we could well have counted and had known rain, hail, shine and, on occasion, moonlight on sundry rock-faces from Buachaille Etive Mor to the surf-ringed cliffs of Cornwall. He claimed to have done the regulation sail up Loch Katrine to Stronachlachar in the tourist steamer *Sir Walter Scott*; otherwise he appeared to be almost as deplorably uneducated as I was. Certainly he seemed to have much to commend him as the ideal companion, the more especially as his wife Alison nobly agreed to meet us with the essential transport at the end of the walk.

We chose a day in mid-October when, fortunately, the weather was at its superlative best. Mais and Kenneth, the youngest member of our family, came with us as support party to Glen Falloch in order to do the very necessary job of taking the car back to base in Helensburgh. For Mais, the cumulative effect of superb autumn colouring and spendthrift morning sun must have made it almost painfully difficult to watch us disembark at Beinn Ghlas farm and prepare to start.

Norman was quickly ready, his only obvious luggage a crook and a paper bag, which I fervently hoped contained food. It is his rooted belief that one should travel light; indeed I have even known him on occasion offer to help a companion to travel equally unencumbered by eating half of the latter's lunch.

"What on earth are you carrying there?" he asked, eyeing my bulging rucksack with ill-disguised scorn. "Are you sure you've put in the distress flares and your spare insoles?"

I treated the question with the contempt it deserved, then hoisted the burden on to my back with as much nonchalance as I could muster. The expedition was ready. The time was 11.15.

From the back of the farm the way climbs steeply for 750 feet, close to the falls which are seen so impressively from the road at Inverarnan. There is no real track, only bits and pieces of paths which zigzag pleasantly upwards through the bracken and scattered trees. Although one gains height rapidly, it is a slightly discouraging start to the day for anyone in poor training, and I found myself taking an increasingly profound interest in the views. These were unforgettable. The autumn colouring was just coming to its best, so that all round us and in the glen at our feet there was a glorious mixture of greens and golds, of reds and browns and yellows. There was scarcely any wind, only peace and serenity everywhere, emphasized by the mirror-waters of the lower reaches of the Falloch. Ben Vorlich, haze-girdled, made the background; centrepiece was the white of Inverarnan Hotel.

We learned afterwards from Mais, who called in to see Nancy and Hannah Girvan, that at that precise time they were at their busiest cleaning and clearing in readiness for the sale of the building.

To those unacquainted with Inverarnan this would mean little; to countless others the event is one that has in it the very substance of history. For Inverarnan Hotel and the kindness of the Girvan family, its owners, have become a saga of Scotland that spans almost forty years. To the cheery lounges and dining-room, and more intimately to 'the den'—the Girvans' own fireside—came three generations of climbers, hill-walkers and skiers. No warmer welcome existed anywhere. Never, at any time, was the most awkward request too much trouble: I can think of nowhere else where, at half-past eleven at night, a ravenous climbing party of four would have been given a full three-course dinner ending up with blaeberries and cream. New Year hospitality—with traditional song and story— was legendary and when, in 1966, winter closing became necessary, it seemed to many of us like the world coming to an end. Now, as Norman and I looked down on the familiar buildings, the saga—although we did not realise it—was being brought inexorably to an end. But whatever the future may hold, the forty years of Inverarnan will live on as one of the happiest chapters in the story of the Scottish hills.

Our upward route took us across the slope almost to the edge of the falls. There was no great volume of water coming down, but we had a number of excellent close-ups of some of the most impressive drops, wild white jets landing on the gleaming rock-shelves below. This is a truly splendid waterfall, adding character to the whole of this lower part of Glen Falloch.

Like so many other Scottish falls, the appearance of the Grey Mare's Tail, as it is sometimes called, alters completely according to the weather conditions: dramatic in the extreme after a spell of heavy rain, vanishing almost to non-existence in times of drought. More than once, during prolonged periods of dry weather, climbs have been done right up the centre line of the fall. The route, according to a former president of the Scottish Mountaineering Club who led a party up some years ago, looks thoroughly formidable from below but is found to be much less exacting on closer acquaintance. Some of the

pitches from cauldron to cauldron are no more than steep
scrambles, and it is only near the final exit that any genuine
difficulty occurs.

When, in September 1803, Dorothy and William Words-
worth climbed up past the falls from Glen Falloch on one of
their marathon walks, they were clearly immensely impressed.
Even without pioneering a new rock-climb up the actual
stream-bed, Dorothy decided that the ascent was "very
laborious, being frequently almost perpendicular", while
William, with the noise of the falls in his ears, was all for calling
Glen Falloch "the Vale of Awful Sound".

Before it takes off on the first of its leaps into space, the
Beinn Ghlas burn is channelled through a deep, rocky gorge.
We followed along the rim of this, gradually gaining height
till we reached the more level moor above. As we paused for a
moment to take stock of our position, we had a memorable
backward glimpse of Beinn Laoigh—its sharp pyramid suddenly
revealed in a V-notch of haze, a light screen behind the horseshoe corrie of the Dubh Eas, 'the black waterfall'; then slowly
the mist rose and once more hid the peak from sight.

We were now faced with the crossing of an extensive desert
of moorland, seemingly unlimited acres of tawny-coloured
grass, where there were no landmarks and where route-finding
in mist would be tricky in the extreme. Our line took us away
from the winding trench of the burn, to the right of Parlan
Hill and up to a low pass crossed by pylons and power lines
which, like ourselves, had climbed up the hillside from Glen
Falloch. Now and again we could hear stags roaring. It was
difficult to decide precisely where the sounds were coming
from, although once we saw three beasts high on the skyline,
close to the summit of Parlan Hill.

The going was exceptionally boggy and wet: now and
again the oozing, slippery mud of peat hags, more often
treacherous moss. Once we flushed a snipe, which zigzagged
away in some disorder, and once Norman, in the full flight of
describing vividly an experimental three-man canoe journey
down the Fal River in Cornwall which ended not surprisingly
upside down, was deceived by a tussock into landing knee-deep
in a morass.

I could not help recalling more than once that we were

still on the route which the Wordsworths had followed, and mentally I accorded Dorothy full marks for her perseverance. "The walk was very laborious," she observed in her *Recollections*, "being often exceedingly stony, or through swampy moss, rushes, or rough heather." Fortunately they seem to have had the services of a first-rate guide. "We were astonished at the sagacity with which our Highlander discovered the track, where often no track was visible to us, and scarcely even when he pointed it out. It reminded us of what we read of the Hottentots and other savages. He went on as confidently as if it had been a turnpike road—the more surprising, as when he was there before it must have been a plain track, for he told us that fishermen from Arrochar carried herrings regularly over the mountains by that way to Loch Ketterine when the glens were much more populous than now."

Norman and I were not sorry when at last we reached the highest point of the pass, some 2 miles from the falls and midway between Parlan Hill on our left and Ben Ducteach on our right. At the summit of the latter three counties meet—Dunbartonshire, Stirlingshire and Perthshire; the rest of our walk would be in Perthshire. The col itself lies on the watershed of Scotland, that line which wanders so intriguingly backwards and forwards up the length of the country. From here its farther course was roughly eastwards, over the tops of the Crianlarich hills, then down the Grey Height of Cruach Ardrain and across the main road to some moorland meanderings and another climb to the more definite ridges of the Beinn Laoigh group.

Curiously enough, although most of the water in the burns would now be flowing to an ultimate destination in the North Sea, much would also be piped off from Loch Katrine down the aqueduct to Glasgow and so, eventually, back to the Atlantic.

We lunched in a sun-trap not far below the head of the pass. It was pleasantly warm, the south-east breeze cooling us off just sufficiently after our exertions on the moor, although a scattering of 'grey mare's tails' in the sky suggested stronger winds in the near future. For welcome to Glen Gyle, a pair of ravens passed overhead, close enough for a good look at the intruders. Norman, I was glad to see, had for once brought an ample lunch with him, not—as I knew was disquietingly liable to happen—a lightweight diet of prunes.

Not far down Glen Gyle we were pleasantly surprised to come on a stony track which followed roughly the direction of the power lines. For a while, too, we noticed Land-Rover tracks which, strangely, seemed to begin and end nowhere. We wondered idly if the vehicle which made them had been dropped by the helicopter we had previously seen being used in the erection of the pylons on the Glen Falloch side of the pass.

Then, quite dramatically round a bluff, we had our first glimpse of Loch Katrine. Unfortunately one of the pylons stuck up exactly in the middle like the proverbial sore thumb, yet even so the view was an impressive one: the loch utterly calm in the windless afternoon and reaching far into the distance; the colourings in the autumn heat-haze soft luminous browns and dark contrasting greens.

Glen Gyle, ancient territory of the MacGregors and birth-place of Rob Roy MacGregor himself, is anything but easy of access. No more than 3 miles long from the summit of our pass to the head of Loch Katrine, it could of course be reached by an alternative route to ours, from the north-east, over the hills from Balquhidder; this, however, looks on the map to be long, wearisome and probably not particularly rewarding. Further-more, in the other direction, unless he has permission the motorist is allowed no nearer than Stronachlachar another 3 miles down the loch, where the run of the steamer *Sir Walter Scott* also ends.

No doubt all this is as it should be, specially designed to foster the feeling of remoteness, already strong; the feeling that this could be the back of beyond, an ideal hideout for cattle-lifters and whence perhaps the war-galleys of Clan Alpin might suddenly emerge, just as Scott pictured them:

> Far up the lengthen'd lake were spied
> Four darkening specks upon the tide,
> That, slow enlarging on the view,
> Four mann'd and masted barges grew,
> And, bearing downwards from Glengyle,
> Steer'd full upon the lonely isle.

Much to our disappointment we could make out no birlinns being launched from any distant strand and the only cattle we saw—a herd which Norman suggested might be Devon-

Highland crosses—had a glow to their sleek russet coats which spoke of complete contentment rather than of the privations of a furtive night-trek over the hills from the lands of some luckless neighbour.

From the lower part of the glen we had a succession of particularly fine views over our shoulders to Ben Ducteach. Although not quite 2,000 feet high, this is a most shapely hill, a succession of black, slabby outcrops, typical of much of the country hereabouts, making a picturesque giant's stairway on its south face. Only the heat-haze and the repeated intrusion of the pylons prevented much dallying for photography. Up on our left the side of the glen lifted steeply to an indeterminate skyline. Catching the full warmth of the afternoon sun, the dead bracken and scattered trees made a magnificent blaze of colour, fully complementary to the shapely hill behind and the first reaches of the loch ahead.

It was, however, in the approaches to Glen Gyle House that we had our most striking foretaste of the autumn splendour that was to be with us now all the way down Loch Katrine. A stretch of the Glen Gyle Water led us into extensive woodland and here the colouring was striking beyond description, chiefly perhaps because of the contrasts—the yellows and golds of the birches offset by the dark greens of the pines, and, intermediate between these extremes, the oaks and occasional larches. It was one of the most variegated colour-shows I have ever seen, immensely worth all the toil that had gone into the long approach march. Here too, at last, we saw a few birds, mostly tits and one or two robins. From now on we were to hear plenty of them, busy among the beeches and birches, and I kept thinking of the choruses there must be in early summer, with the migrants at their most exuberant. Once we saw a heron on leisurely passage out towards one of the islands and later we heard the irritable chatter of a jay or a magpie among some firs, but on the whole the day's total was not outstanding.

Through the trees we had nearer views of the loch, unruffled in the afternoon sunshine. Far different, I reflected, must have been the moods which inspired one possible meaning of the name—'the loch of the furies' or 'fiends'—said to derive from the old Welsh word, *cethern*. Another interpretation is, of course, the 'cateran' (freebooter) loch which, if correct, would be especially interesting, as the name goes back at least as far as the mid-fifteenth century, quite a while before Rob Roy's day (1671–1734).

So far we had covered 5¼ miles and seemed to be satisfactorily up to schedule. Another 8 miles, the full length of the loch, lay ahead and this, rather to our surprise, now promised to be along an immaculate tarmac road.

At first, after the bogs alongside the burn, the tarmac seemed an excellent idea: if we had only to follow this to journey's end then the day's work was virtually over. How wrong we were! How very far wrong! Long before the 8 miles were finished we were to be fully convinced that we were in fact slogging barefoot over red-hot ploughshares. So at least it seemed to me—and I have a sneaking feeling that Norman felt much the same—for the wet going earlier in the day had ensured a softening up process for my heels and toes in preparation for every monotonous, jarring step on the road. It was not to be long before I was in the throes of the most painful skinning and blistering I can remember.

To begin with, of course, this was no hindrance to appreciating the beauty of the loch. Sometimes we walked through long avenues of trees, with shafts of sunlight streaming through; then the road would climb to give us more open views of the succession of bays and headlands. Unfortunately, when looking across the loch, we were facing directly into the sun and could thus see very few details of the far side; even the pattern of islands was difficult to make out against the background dazzle of haze. Once, after a higher climb than usual, we passed a noisy gathering of sheep, where half a dozen men with their dogs were busy at the autumn dipping. We were given a wave and a cheery greeting. It would be warm work for them, we decided, although, with its open sunny outlook, in one of the finest situations imaginable.

For more than 100 years Loch Katrine has been Glasgow's main—and justly famous—water-supply. Largely because of this its privacy has been jealously guarded, so that except to hill-walkers and to those familiar with the access points at the Trossachs and Stronachlachar, it is not particularly well known. Anywhere else the excellent motor road which we were following would have been intolerably busy with cars; as it was, we saw no more than perhaps half a dozen along the whole of the 8-mile stretch. Naturally the farther we walked and the more superheated our feet became, the harder it was to be strong-minded and resist the temptation of trying to thumb a lift. Once when we heard a van coming up behind us, I made a heartrending appeal to Norman with the plea that I thought the time really had come, but he walked on heedless, in flinty, impassive silence. There are some occasions on which I find Norman's personality less radiant than on others.

On the south side of the loch Ben Venue (2,393 feet) was gradually bulking more prominently in the view. It is a fine hill and a particularly good viewpoint, as Norman and I had learnt for ourselves when we climbed it with Theo Nicholson back in 1948. It would be difficult all the same to match some of the descriptions of it given by the writer of *The Scottish Tourist* of 1825: his regrets, for instance, that "much of the wood has been cut down which gave so much of picturesque effect to Benvenue, clothing him to the shoulders in a green robe, through the openings of which, rocks appeared like targe and breastplate, while they gave unspeakable grace to his descending skirts, as they recede, in lessening folds, along the western shore of the lake".

Of Ben A'an, on the other side of the Trossachs, he waxes no less eloquent: "North-east of Benvenue, and distant about a mile and a half, Ben-an lifts his white top 1800 feet above the level of the sea, a perfect pinnacle, and for the last 400 or 500 feet apparently inaccessible. In his ample sides are dingle and bushy dell. Though his crest is cleft with lightning, he listens to the 'crash of thunder, and the warring winds' without dismay; and exposing his bare forehead to the tempest's shock, grimly guards the pass 'like a veteran gray in arms'." Ben A'an is in fact a most shapely little hill, much in favour on account of its readily accessible rock-climbs, and it formed an ideal complement to Ben Venue in our views ahead towards the Trossachs.

As we came slowly nearer to the foot of the loch, we kept looking more and more often to see if we could make out the waiting red Mini, the end of all our labours. At last a shout from Norman proclaimed that he had seen it, half-hidden among some trees near the jut of a dark promontory. At once our step acquired a new spring, my limping became noticeably more sprightly. We waved joyfully to herald our imminent arrival. Alas for our optimism, the red object which Norman had glimpsed was not the Mini after all but merely the shell of a derelict tractor; there was still another three-quarters of a mile to go.

The sun was low now and the late afternoon agreeably cool. Against the silhouette of Ben Venue the final stretch of the loch was black and narrow as a river. Tied up at the pier on the far side, the *Sir Walter Scott* lay deserted and silent, a pale ghost of a ship. Everywhere it was absolutely still, the only sound the falls of an artificial inlet we had passed some time back, magnified out of proportion by the encroaching walls of trees.

And then at length we really were at the end of the loch. And there was the Mini waiting invitingly for us, fortunately for my blisters at the nearest point of the enormous car-park. Already Alison was busy with a thermos flask, pouring out cups of the most welcome tea I have ever tasted.

It was exactly six o'clock. We had taken $6\frac{3}{4}$ hours for the whole walk—not a very commendable time when compared with the 5 hours and 7 minutes we should have needed according to the well-known formula (an hour for every 3 miles, plus half an hour for every 1,000 feet of climbing). Though how, I ventured to wonder, can a long day of peerless autumn sunshine really be reduced to a mathematical formula?

Sir Walter Scott tells how in the old days, before the road through the Trossachs was made, "there was no mode of issuing out of the defile excepting by a sort of ladder, composed of the branches and roots of trees". Perhaps, if it had been as difficult as all that, I might not have bothered to try. And yet, looking back, I do not think that even a barrier as formidable as that would have stopped me. For I had a very shrewd idea, amply borne out in the event, of just how good the Easton hospitality would be as memorable climax to the day at their familiar house near Killearn.

The Loch

Had Loch Lomond been in a happier climate, it would have been the boast of wealth and vanity to own one of the little spots which it incloses, and to have employed upon it all the arts of embellishment. But as it is, the islets, which court the gazer at a distance, disgust him at his approach, when he finds, instead of soft lawns and shady thickets, nothing more than uncultivated ruggedness.

Dr. Samuel Johnson

FOR three days there had been keen frost, with belts of fog, cold, clammy and persistent. But now the thaw had set in and as the temperature rose there was a kindlier warmth in the intermittent November sun: already it had turned the hoar-frost on trees and hedges to millions of silver drops; away beyond the copper of the moors thin clouds had gathered to hide the highest of Ben Lomond's snow-dusting.

My daughter Helen and I were on our way to Balmaha and our spirits lifted in keeping with the gay autumn colouring. Our hopes were high that the weather would remain fair, for we were looking forward keenly to the repetition of a familiar pleasure—accompanying Mr. Alick Macfarlane, Loch Lomond island postman, on one of his morning rounds.

Ever since May 1948 Alick has run the official postal service to the islands, using his well-known boatyard at Balmaha as base. Summer and winter, year in year out, he has kept the service going, making his circuit on two mornings a week, Mondays and Thursdays, all the year round, and adding a further run on Saturdays during the summer months. The inhabitants of the islands certainly have good reason to be thankful for this change from the old days, when they had to fetch their own mail from the mainland.

First to greet us at the boatyard was Sally, the alsatian. Sally is Alick's constant companion, accompanying him— usually with Susie the cairn terrier as well—on all his trips as crew-member; indeed it would perhaps be more accurate to describe her as skipper, for once the launch is under way she gives a very fair impression of having taken over command. She does the rounds repeatedly and with obvious efficiency, pausing only for an occasional cockpit conference, or at the tip of the bow to cast a dignified glance around to make sure that everything on board is shipshape.

"Glad to see you again," came Alick's cheerful welcome from the black maw of the repair shed. "And it's just as well you didn't choose yesterday; visibility in that fog was down to 20 yards."

We were not slow to agree. Looking across the dancing ripples of the loch and up at the pools of blue sky, we had good reason to be grateful for the bright change in the weather.

The *Lady Jean*, the launch used during the winter months, was lying alongside the narrow wooden jetty, her red and white Royal Mail burgee fluttering gently at the masthead. With Sally and Susie leading the way, we were all quickly aboard, Alick with a not very fat post-pouch slung over his shoulder.

"You'll need to come again next month," he laughed, no doubt guessing our thoughts. "There'll be plenty of mail then. During Christmas week we actually have to have five runs; the letters and parcels are like an avalanche. There must be people all over the world imagining their friends on the islands here are starving."

It was good to be enjoying once again a glimpse of that familiar pawky humour which has gone to the building of his postman's popularity over so many hundreds of island runs.

The engine fired without protest and within a few minutes we were sweeping out of the anchorage—oddly unfamiliar without the usual congestion and bustle of summer. We rounded the point into open water and met the breeze, blowing down the long miles of the loch, ice-keen as though straight from the snows on Ben Lomond. On our left the dense wood-jungle of Inchcailleach climbed sharply for 200 feet: oak and larch, rowan and birch, alder and fir and pine, massed in sumptuous late autumn colouring against the rust of the dead bracken.

Inchcailleach owes its name, 'isle of old women', to the nunnery which was on it long ago. Nowadays it is one of the five islands which, along with part of the mainland shore and the marshy ground on the south side of the River Endrick, go to make up the Loch Lomond nature reserve. The other islands—Torrinch, Creinch, Clairinch and the Aber Isle—are all much smaller, but together form a barrier screen across the mouth of the Endrick.

No one lives on Inchcailleach now, although in summer it is often more than busy with picnickers, and our first call of the morning was farther on, at Inchfad, 'the long island'. We reached it within seven minutes of leaving Balmaha, slowing gently to a stop at the jetty, almost on the doorstep of the trim white farmhouse with its adjacent steading. It was on Inchfad, Alick will tell you, round about the middle of the eighteenth century, that his great-great-grandfather Duncan used to distil whisky—perfectly legally. Indeed it is not so very long since bits and pieces of the old still were to be seen and if one knew where to look, traces of the site could be made out on the ground.

First delivery and cheery exchange of greetings over, we moved out once again, on a long reverse curve, then headed for the north-east tip of the island. Once round the point the *Lady Jean* met the full force of the wind. Flurries of spray, freezing cold, whipped into our faces as the bow slapped through the waves. Crest and furrow reached confusedly ahead as we made now towards Inchcruin, 'the round island', once used, according to one old guide-book, as an asylum for the insane. Lying off to starboard like the hump of some ungainly monster, was Bucinch, the bushy little 'island of goats'.

For a little we gave ourselves over to sheer luxury—to the fresh breeze, to the feel of the sun, to the tonic invigoration of the spray. This, surely, was what we had come for; for the feeling of spaciousness that reached far beyond the loch's bounding trees and rocks and shingle. Far ahead, the narrows between Ben Lomond and the Glen Douglas hills seemed to be issuing an invitation to go sailing on, always a little farther from the commonplace world that we had just left behind. There is indeed always something particularly satisfying about a good day such as this spent out of doors in the middle of winter. It is like an unexpected bonus, as though one had been allowed an extra bit of summer as part of the wages of virtue.

Looking across the foot of Glen Falloch to Inverarnan and the Beinn Ghlas falls

(overleaf)
A part of the Beinn Ghlas falls above Glen Falloch

The half-day sail we were enjoying is available to anyone for the asking, and we could not help wondering why it is that so many city-dwellers seem to be perennially content to put up with hibernation at the tail end of the year. November and December can offer wonderful days quite unguessed at in the murk of the town—days with the woods still aflame with autumn's dying, with fresh snow on the hills and with a clarity in the views unknown in the muggy warmth of July or August.

We were fortunate to have been given just such a morning, and as the wind sang in our ears with the *Lady Jean*'s progress, we were duly grateful. Steadily the scattered trees and shingle edging of Inchfad dropped astern.

All the time Sally, the alsatian, kept restlessly on the go, pushing past us on her tours of inspection, cocking her head each time she paused beside her master to listen attentively to anything he had to say.

"Doesn't she ever fall overboard?" asked Helen. "She must find things a bit awkward when it's rough."

"She did once," replied Alick thoughtfully. "I didn't notice at first either. It was drizzling at the time, with everything very slippery and she must have skidded off the stern. Luckily she fell clear of the screw." He paused for a moment to light a fresh cigarette. "I noticed after a bit, of course, and turned back to look for her, though I was sure she must be lost. At first I couldn't see her at all, then I spotted the tips of her ears above the water. There she was, paddling away quite the thing, making for one of the islands. I had a mighty hard job getting her aboard, as I was alone, of course, and she's heavy enough even when she's not soaking wet. She swam twice round the boat, too, not wanting to come back aboard. I think she imagined she would be in for a thundering good row. Isn't that right, Sally?" But Sally was away again on yet another tour, just to make sure that everything up for'ard was entirely to her liking.

Away beyond Bucinch, a good three-quarters of a mile to the north, a sudden dazzle of sunlight was playing tricks with the colouring of one of the most beautiful of all Loch Lomond's islands, Inchlonaig, 'isle of yew trees'. Against the background russet and white of the Ben, its wooded knolls flashed out of cloud-shadow into a gay pattern of golds and greens and

(overleaf)
The jetty, Inchmurrin. Alick Macfarlane and the Margaret

Pink-footed geese near Loch Leven

browns. There stood the one white house, unoccupied and solitary during the 'off' season, flanked by numerous bottle-green blobs—the thickly clustered yew trees which gave the island its name. These trees have a place in Scottish history, for it is said that they were planted on the instructions of Robert the Bruce to supply bows for his fighting men.

Four and a half centuries later, in 1773, Inchlonaig was probably one of the islands on which Johnson and Boswell landed after their Hebridean tour, while they were breaking their southward journey at Rossdhu.

> From Glencroe [wrote the Doctor] we passed through a pleasant country to the banks of Loch Lomond, and were received at the house of Sir James Colquhoun, who is owner of almost all the thirty islands of the loch, which we went in a boat next morning to survey. The heaviness of the rain shortened our voyage, but we landed on one island planted with yew, and stocked with deer, and on another containing perhaps not more than half an acre, remarkable for the ruins of an old castle, on which the osprey builds her annual nest.

According to the familiar story, the worthy Doctor was not particularly popular when he returned to Rossdhu from this boating excursion. He was soaked to the skin and is said to have entered the drawing-room with water spouting from his boots, whereupon Lady Colquhoun could not help exclaiming: "What a bear!"

"Yes," replied one of the company present, "he is no doubt a bear, but it is Ursa Major."

Once past the northern tip of Inchcruin, Alick swung the *Lady Jean* to port into the shallow backwater known to fisher-men as 'The Geggles', a square-shaped lagoon more or less enclosed by Inchcruin, Inchmoan and Inchconnachan. For the newcomer it is a puzzling place, with few distinctive landmarks, a place where it is extraordinarily difficult to keep a sense of direction; indeed, the first time we had been taken through I had decided that route-finding on the hills was child's play by comparison. And just how Alick had worried his way by compass through the grey void of the previous day's fog was a mystery, steering clear of disaster on one of the numerous shingle spits or, equally likely, among the trailing branches of a tree.

Mostly the lagoon is a place of peace and quiet. Canoeists from Rowardennan know it well. Week-enders from Balloch or Balmaha come over in their outboards or cabin cruisers, finding a seclusion in bays and creeks that can compare strangely with the interminable traffic worry only a mile away on the main Loch Lomond road. But as we saw it this November day it was deserted. There was no blue spiral of camp-fire smoke, no tent half-seen in any of the clearings. The level of the loch was high and the branches of waterside trees, gnarled and sinuous, sagged half-submerged, suggestive of riverbanks in the jungle. Surprised by our approach, a party of mallard took off in wild commotion. As we looked back over the stern at the froth and bubble of the *Lady Jean*'s wake, and at the background screening pines, it seemed as though we were a thousand miles from the humdrum round of the city.

Inchmoan, as its name of 'moss island' or 'peat island' suggests, is flat and desolate. It is uninhabited although at one time it provided peat supplies for Luss village. Much more attractive is the mile-long island which flanks the narrow strait to the west, Inchtavannach. Here St. Kessog, the saint of the district, had his retreat, and a man of excellent discrimination he must have been, too, for in the length and breadth of Scotland he could scarcely have found a more delectable place in which to spend his days and nights of prayer and meditation.

Perhaps something of Kessog's influence lingered on in the custom which is recorded in an old guide-book of the eighteenth century: "Concerning Inchtavannach," it says, "they tell us a very curious anecdote, viz. That formerly a bell was suspended on the summit of its highest rock, which, by its ringing, served to warn at the same time the inhabitants of the three adjacent parishes, Luss, Buchanan and Kilmaronock to attend divine service."

Nowadays no bell sounds on 'the monk's island'. The one house is inhabited, however, all the year round, and our welcome, as we drew in to the jetty to hand over the mail, was warm and friendly. But, as at Inchfad, the stop was short. After only a brief exchange of news we reversed away once again, to swing boldly southwards into more open water. Inchtavannach dropped quickly astern, giving way on the other beam to the minute islet of Inch Galbraith, the site, it is said, of an ancient lake dwelling. Now it stands out as a grey rock topped by grey ruins, for on it is the shell of a castle that once was a Galbraith stronghold.

As we moved out now to the widest part of the loch—5 miles from west shore to east—we shivered to the touch of the wind. It seemed to have backed strongly since we left Balmaha and to be funnelling down through the clefts of Glen Luss and Glen Finlas, hissing and singing in the spray that was flicked at our faces by the bow of the *Lady Jean*. Up on the hills shafts of sunshine highlighted each ridge and fold and corrie, but there was a harshness in the play of light in keeping with the slate cloud-pall which had gathered behind us on Ben Lomond. Snow was not far away. Instinctively we huddled round the engine-casing for a little extra warmth.

"The coldest day on the loch I've ever known," began Alick, stowing away the logbook, which he had been meticulously entering up, "was in winter once when we were taking some workmen up to Inversnaid for towing a barge back to Balmaha. There was a full gale blowing from the north, with heavy squalls of snow, and up near the head of the loch we suddenly had a succession of those waterspouts you get about here sometimes. One of them lifted a coil of manila rope we had lying aft, clean off the deck, and whisked it overboard, where, of course, it got tangled solid round the screw."

He broke off for a moment to pull his coat-collar more closely about his ears.

"Luckily," he continued, "we drifted into shallow water and went aground; if we'd gone the other way the boat would have been a complete write-off. I had to jump in up to my waist and cut the rope free with a knife one of the workmen had with him. I remember we had the local blacksmith with us—he'd come for the pleasure of the sail!—and he vowed he'd never come again. It must have been the difference from his forge. Well, would you believe it, when we tried to brew up for tea, the bottom fell out of the kettle, and then someone knocked over the pot with the soup in it. It took us four hours to get back home and it was pitch dark, too. I'd never been so cold in my life before and I was sure I was going to die. But, you know, I didn't."

It is a 3-mile run from Inchtavannach to the next port of call at the southern tip of Inchmurrin. Here the loch is so exposed that on a wild winter's day it can be fiercely rough, too rough indeed on occasion for the mail-run to be risked at all. Even as we saw it, deserted save for a few shy mallard and a solitary incongruous cormorant, we could appreciate how hostile it might be; it was much more difficult to picture the lazy calm of summer, with the yachts and the cabin cruisers, the canoes and the rowing-boats, and—here following her time-honoured track from Balloch to Luss—the *Maid of the Loch* with her jolly throng of trippers.

As we ran down the long mile and a half of Inchmurrin, Alick kept edging the *Lady Jean* gently inshore. Soon we were passing under the ivy-tangle of the old castle and almost immediately the wheel was set spinning to bring us round into the south-western bay. On the southern skyline, gaunt and naked in the notch of the Vale of Leven, stood two tall chimney stalks.

"There's Balloch for you," commented Alick with a grin, "but maybe you'll not really be wanting to look much at it."

We agreed. There were other, more important things to take up our attention: for one, the old cock pheasant strolling bold as brass along the shingle beach; for another, Mr. Tom Scott, proprietor on Inchmurrin, coming down the jetty to greet us.

Inchmurrin is a hospitable island. No wonder Alick always stops there on his postal rounds for a half hour that is apt to have in it more than a little of West Highland elasticity. For his passengers it is a grand opportunity to enjoy a walk or—even more popular—a cup of coffee or a dram. On this occasion Helen and I were made to feel particularly welcome. We had certainly not been expected, yet Mr. Scott set off at once to arrange with his wife to have us suitably entertained. Meanwhile Alick went visiting on his own, while Sally, equally pleased to be ashore, set about her favourite pastime of stalking fieldmice.

To pass the time until coffee was ready, Helen and I climbed the slanting muddy path that leads to the old keep, now no more than a pathetic fragment of what it had once been. Grey, crumbled walls top a grassy hillock, one solitary arched window still standing to lend the place a kind of forlorn dignity, its slot framing the Luss hills and the loch-avenue that leads still farther back to the Ben itself. The historian of the party told me that it was here in this ancient Lennox stronghold, during the reign of James I, that the Duchess of Albany had spent her tragic latter years. After her husband, her two sons and her father had all been executed on the Heading Hill at Stirling, she became a recluse and made this quiet island sanctuary her home.

From the antiquity of the keep to the modernity of the tea-room it was an easy change, a short stroll taking us across to the house where we were to enjoy our interlude of warmth and luxury. Tigh na Camus, as it is called—'the house of the bay' or 'harbour'—is a handsome modern building, complete with cocktail lounge and bedrooms for a small number of visitors. With shingle beach and jetty right on its front doorstep and all Inchmurrin a spacious playground to the rear, it must be a delightful place for a summer-time break; on this November morning, away from the nagging wind and with the big windows receptive to every sun-blink, it had an air of complete unreality.

To complete our enjoyment Mrs. Scott plied us with coffee and biscuits in front of a big log fire, telling us at the same time something of life on the island—not always without its problems, especially so far as schooling and morning transport is concerned. At times, in fact, the streets of town actually seemed quite homely and likeable by comparison.

The sunshine we had felt through the windows of the lounge had been deceptive, for as soon as we re-emerged the cold hit us as sharply as ever. We strolled down to the wooden jetty. Inchmurrin's peace and quiet wrapped us round, the mainland shore opposite—dark green woods up-tilted on the slopes behind Boturich and Balloch—seeming 100 rather than a mere one or 2 miles away. It was our only regret that we had no time left to appreciate more fully the island's out-of-the-world seclusion.

We were ready waiting for Alick as he brought round the *Lady Jean* from our original landing-point to pick us up. We lost no time in going aboard, watched critically by Sally from her commanding vantage-point at the bow. Backing out, we were soon homeward bound, running closely parallel to the brown and green patchwork of the shoreline trees.

My daughter and I agreed afterwards that we had both enjoyed the final lap back to Balmaha best of the whole trip. It was comparatively short, lasting no more than half an hour; the course we followed along the southern fringe of the islands was uncomplicated, arrow-straight; the weather was changing very obviously for the worse—yet in the run, unmistakably, were all the best ingredients of the day's pleasure.

Alick, hunched characteristically at the wheel as the wind sang over the windscreen, reached new heights of brilliance as a story-teller. He told us of his other launches, the *Margaret*, from St. Monance, and the *Marion*, half as fast again, built in Norway in 1939 and a veteran of war service. He had tales of the roe deer and the red deer that live beside the loch and on one or two of the islands, of how they move around, sometimes swimming from island to island in search of better grazing. With vast enjoyment he described some of the amusing situations he had found himself in on days when blanketing mist made route-finding a game of flukes; and eloquently he told of the year of the bitter February frost when the ice was so thick that the *Lady Jean* had to be fitted out as an ice-breaker and even then damaged her screw and rudder and keel. There seemed to be no end to his anecdotes, no bounds to the dry humour of their telling.

In particular we enjoyed the episodes of his own family history, going back to that great-great-grandfather who had spent his time distilling whisky on Inchfad. Next in succession, another Duncan had worked as a cobbler in Balmaha and also as collector of duty from the distilleries of the neighbourhood. Then his son, Alick's grandfather, became bargemaster to the Duke of Montrose, in addition owning his own sailing lighter, which carried birchwood from the upper reaches of the loch to Paisley for use in the manufacture of bobbins; on the return journey coal would usually be the cargo, the barge being traced up the River Leven from the Clyde. Sailing was now obviously in the Macfarlane blood and after going deep sea in the eighties, Alick's father John became yachtmaster to the Duke. A rowing-boat had been purchased for hiring as far back as 1850, and John, in 1915, bought the first family motor-boat, *Water Witch*. Now one of Alick's two sons, Barry, is following in his father's footsteps to continue the long tradition.

We ran past Creinch, 'the tree island', and its outlying rock fragment, where the cormorants like to congregate for their winter fishing; then slightly longer Torrinch, 'the tower island', named after the sheer rock-face on its western shore. Half a mile beyond we were in the gut between Clairinch—rich with its holly in winter, in spring a mass of primroses and hyacinths— and the more familiar woods of Inchcailleach. The *Lady Jean* had all but completed the long third line of the triangle.

Behind us, the sky was still bright, with a few tattered strips of blue, silver-edged. Away beyond the tumbling white furrow of our wake, beyond Inchmurrin, the moors of Beinn Buidhe caught glinting sunlight that set their colours on fire. But ahead, by way of contrast, the sky had been darkening steadily. A black screen of cloud, snow-charged, had spread down the east side of the loch. Ben Lomond and its outlying ridges had been blotted out; then in a moment Conic Hill itself, immediately behind Balmaha, had disappeared. Now and again sudden flurries of hail struck at us, bursts of whirling ice-spicules that spun like dervishes across the troubled grey of the loch and faded again in lulls of comparative calm. We were glad of Inchcailleach's shelter on the final run in to the anchorage.

"Well, come again soon," smiled Alick as we said goodbye on the jetty, leaving him to a final tidying of the launch and the completion of his logbook entries. "I'll expect you anyway, Helen, to come and give me a hand with those Christmas mails. It won't be long now till we start making our extra runs."

As we sprinted to the car through a further venomous on-slaught of hail, we both knew for sure that this was one invitation we were not going to turn down.

12

The Snows

"These—these—are very awkward skates; ain't they, Sam?"
inquired Mr. Winkle, staggering.

"I'm afeerd there's a orkard gen'l'm'n in 'em, sir," replied
Sam.

Charles Dickens

Up in the North-east it had been a particularly hard winter.
Blizzard after blizzard had swept the high ground, piling the
snow-beds in the corries to immense depths and leaving few
bald patches on the upper ridges. Even at lower levels in
Banffshire and Aberdeenshire the snow-ploughs had been
heavily overworked and almost as far down as the Moray coast
roadside drifts and white fields had come to be accepted as
normal.

There was, in short, no excuse. The time had come to
remove the rust and dust from my equipment and realise an
ambition of long standing—one of those ambitions that have
a particularly strong appeal when considered from the depths
of an armchair—a crossing of the Cairngorms on skis.

Let it be quite clear from the start that my career as a skier
has been almost wholly undistinguished. The only brief
moments of glory to have brightened the drabness came in the
early months of the war, in 1940, when in a sudden access of
folly I volunteered for the ski-battalion that was being raised
by the Scots Guards to go and join the fight against the Russians
in Finland. The adjutant, an outspoken type, told me bluntly
at the preliminary interview: "Well, we certainly wouldn't have
anyone with less ski-ing experience than you." In the event,
however, he was sufficiently kind-hearted to accept me and as
a result I had a delightful week of ski-ing at Chamonix, before
the battalion, after a night in Glasgow on board the troopship
Batory, was finally disbanded at Bordon.

After this meteor-flash of brilliance obscurity supervened once
more. Indeed in all likelihood there would never have been

anything further to add, had it not been for my friend Theo Nicholson.

Almost always on our numerous climbing expeditions together Theo and I would talk over future ploys on the hills. One of these had been a plan for a long day on skis, well away from the crowds and of course as we pictured it, with snow and weather conditions at their idyllic best. It was quite early on that I had ventured to suggest a crossing of the Cairngorms.

The most remarkable thing about this idea was that Theo should ever have given it a second thought. His ski-ing experience is immense, ranging from the Canadian Rockies through Britain and most of the Alps to the farthest corners of Scandinavia, and the prospect of crawling across the plateau of the Cairngorms in company with a particularly lame duck can only have filled him with dismay. However, even after a day on Meall a' Bhuiridh, in Glencoe, when he had ample opportunity to see me at my worst, he still managed to say he thought the scheme was a good one. This, I decided, was chivalry at its finest.

We managed eventually to get down to actual planning, noting with a good deal of alarm how quickly the expedition seemed to assume the appearance of a full-scale military operation.

The route itself was soon agreed on. From the Linn of Dee, 6 miles from Braemar, it would lie west then north-west to take in three summits, all of which would be new to me at least—Carn Cloich-mhuillin (3,087 feet), Beinn Bhrotain (3,795 feet) and Monadh Mor (3,651 feet); it would then cross the expanse of the Great Moss and, cutting over the shoulder of Carn Ban Mor (3,443 feet) not far south of the cairn, would drop finally to Achlean farm in Glen Feshie. The total distance would be some 20 miles and there would be rather more than 3,500 feet of climbing.

These details were perfectly simple. There were, however, complications of our own making, for we debated whether, if weather conditions were unfavourable, it might not be advisable to do the crossing in the reverse direction—roughly north-south instead of south-north. This introduced a new element into our planning which was not at all helpful, and before we knew quite what had happened we found ourselves in a mist of uncertainty. Long-range forecasts, 'highs' and 'lows' over Greenland or Scandinavia, probable and improbable snow conditions—the more we thought about what we might meet, the more unsettling it all became. We took our problem to the met. men and they could not have tried to be more helpful, but they were also extremely cautious in their more distant forecasting and it was clear that in the last resort the success of the project must depend on our own judgment— aided, no doubt, by a dash of good luck.

At times, too, the make-up of the party seemed to be as variable as the weather itself. Several friends were keen to come with us, but it was quite impossible to find dates to suit everyone and in the end all that was left was a quartet of age and youth: Theo and his son John, a friend of the latter, Robert Dean, and myself. With John and Robert at that time still at school at Gordonstoun and Theo at home in Cheshire, the co-ordination of our planning was not of the easiest.

Yet another major problem was transport. It would be simple enough to reach either of our possible starting-points, on Deeside or in Glen Feshie, but it would be quite another matter while we were actually on the march to have the cars spirited round to the other side of the Cairngorms—100 miles away by road—there to meet us and carry us back to the flesh-pots. In the end it was Theo's wife Thelma who saved the day. She volunteered most generously to come on the expedition as driver, and when, following her lead, a second car complete with schoolboy driver was promised from Gordonstoun, we felt we could sit back and relax.

Gradually all the various details were settled, and when at last the met. office ventured a more confident prediction of a spell of cold, bright weather with winds light to moderate veering north-east, we actually went so far as to name the day. Our initial south-north choice, Deeside to Speyside, seemed the more sensible direction after all, with the Cairngorm Club hut at Muir of Inverey near Braemar an obviously excellent starting-point. There was no longer any hope of a reprieve.

Or, as my daughter happily put it: "It'll be a wonderful trip to describe, Dad. If you survive."

As Theo, Thelma and I turned off the road to the cottage at

Muir of Inverey, the sun was already setting in frosty splendour. It had been a day of no wind and remarkably little cloud, and as we drove north through the length of Perthshire and into Aberdeenshire, our spirits had been justifiably high. The road over the Devil's Elbow and the Cairnwell had been ice-free, but on the hills round about the sparkling snowfields and well-filled corries had given promise of great things for the morrow. For Theo perhaps, with his ample experience of cross-country travel in Norway, it would be a day of negligible significance, but so far as I was concerned it was to be an introduction to mountain touring on a bigger scale than I had known before, to the one side of ski-ing which had always had outstanding appeal. The long, clear views had seemed somehow prophetic; now, more prosaically, as we busied ourselves unloading skis and rucksacks from the car, opening up the cottage and fetching pine-logs for the stove, we could feel the sudden bitterness of the frost. Ears and fingertips were quickly chilled and in the keen air the least sound carried far.

There is nothing at all spartan about the Muir of Inverey cottage-hut. Once the coal and pine-log stove is well alight, the spacious kitchen-livingroom becomes a place of real comfort. An electric cooker, a hot water immerser and well-equipped cupboards make cooking simple, while in the dormitories there are even heaters available in case taking to one's bunk should be altogether too chilly to endure.

It was long after dark when the Gordonstoun boys arrived. They burst upon us as we sat in a genial fug at the stove, doing our best to digest a culinary masterpiece of Theo's which can only be described as a horsey hoosh. They exuded energy and enthusiasm, the driver, Adam Acworth, making light of their 100 miles of snow-choked roads and darkness. Their first requirement seemed to be an enormous meal, so we watched them getting down to that in earnest, then, long before they were finished, yawned our own way off to bed.

Next morning there was a scattering of cloud about, but it had done nothing to lessen the intense cold, and we agreed that it looked certain to clear later. Theo had whipped us into a shuffle of activity around 5.30 a.m., but a further hour and a half had gone by before we were finished with breakfast and had loaded the Gordonstoun car with our equipment. Adam was going to drive us to our starting-point at the Linn of Dee, one valuable mile on our way.

This was not, of course, a luxury which could be spun out for very long; in less than five minutes we were piling out again under the pines. Before us stretched the track to the White Bridge, unusable by car by reason of the padlocked gate which barred the way.

As we decked ourselves out beneath ungainly loads of skis, ski-sticks and rucksacks, each of us seemed to look more incongruous than his neighbour. Theo, unselfish as usual, had burdened himself with the communal ice-axe which we had decided to take, and the sight of this, sticking up out of his rucksack, provoked his son to unseemly mirth.

"I say, Dad," came the irreverent remark, "you look like a submarine."

"And I jolly well feel like one too," came back the rejoinder from somewhere out of unseen depths. I could not find it in my heart to add the comments of my own which I felt like making on the subject of Theo's cap. It was one that had been picked up at a sale for 1s. 6d. and thereafter—whether by mistake or as a protective measure I never could discover—had been boiled in eucalyptus oil. The trouble was that it looked like it too.

It was a delightful walk of fifty-five minutes to the White Bridge. The road had an honest sandy surface and at first we felt out of luck that we had not been able to obtain permission to use the car; farther on, however, we changed our tune, for increasingly numerous snow-drifts, iron hard, presented obstacles that would obviously have caused a great deal of trouble. In any case it was much too enjoyable an introduction for us to have the least regrets. It was good just to be alive on such a morning. The air was keen, heady, exhilarating, our pace nicely judged to warm us to the day's work. Close to the track we saw several small parties of stags and hinds, their colouring blending closely with the tawny-browns of the hillsides. Down by the Dee, where occasional ice-floes drifted past, oyster-catchers went piping over the shingle-spits, while now and again a grouse whirred clacking from the heather—cheerful reminders of the bird-song we might have been enjoying hereabouts, had this been May or June.

Of the higher hills we had poor views: nothing more interesting than those humps beside the upper Geldie, Carn Ealar and An Sgarsoch. But after a couple of miles the dull moors on our right fell back and there, quite suddenly, was our shapely first top, Carn Cloich-mhuillin, with a great white billow behind it, frozen into immobility at the moment of breaking—the summit crest of Beinn Bhrotain. Up there lay our route.

Situated at an altitude of 1,336 feet, the White Bridge is not actually white, but grey; solid wooden superstructure on solid stone piers. Just before it is reached a signpost marks the parting of the ways, one green arm pointing right, to Aviemore via the Lairig Ghru, the other across the bridge, to Glen Tilt and Glen Feshie.

We were to see something of Glen Tilt as we went on our way, now following the farther bank of the Dee on short, crisp heather. It featured prominently in our backward views, a deep trench cut below the snow-plastering of Beinn a' Ghlo and leading back, it seemed to suggest, to the warmer, friendlier country of the South.

It was not far from here, in the year 1749, that one of a detachment of English soldiers stationed near the White Bridge was murdered. A few years later two Highlanders were arrested for the crime and taken to Edinburgh for trial at the High Court. The proceedings went forward with due solemnity until the chief witness for the prosecution told how he had seen and talked with the English soldier's ghost, and so learnt the names of the murderers.

"And what language was it that he talked?" he was asked by the defending advocate.

"As good Gaelic as myself," came the answer. And the case ended in unexpected mirth.

After a quarter of a mile we left the river-bank and made straight for the top of Carn Cloich-mhuillin, still almost 3 miles away. The going remained mostly over heather, for so far these south-facing slopes were not high enough to carry more than patches of snow. Our skis at this time, bowing us down and chafing our shoulders, seemed so much unnecessary lumber. Fortunately, however, the weather could scarcely have been kinder, with little or no wind and a mother-of-pearl sky that gave promise of even better things to come. Now opening out north-eastwards, the gateway to the Lairig—on the one side the Devil's Point and on the other Carn a' Mhaim—had all the impressive grandeur of a high Alpine pass.

The sun burst through as we approached the top of Carn Cloich-mhuillin, performing, with sudden generosity, a miracle of colour transformation. In the granite of the boulders and screes we discovered shell-pink and coral and sandy-brown; in the lichens, yellows and greens and greys. New gaiety swept across the moors below, and against the spreading blue above, the upper snowfields of Beinn Bhrotain and Ben Macdhui stretched long arcs of silver.

We were thankful all the same for a lazy quarter of an hour at the cairn. We lay back satisfied and enjoyed the far views: Lochnagar and the Ben Uarns, the Blair Atholl hills, Ben Alder and Creag Meaghaidh, possibly even Ben Nevis in the distant jumble of Lochaber. We looked down too on the head-waters of the Feshie and the Geldie, running almost parallel within a stone's throw of each other, yet the one flowing to the Spey, the other to the Dee. This bleak bit of moorland must surely be quite the loneliest stretch of the Aberdeenshire-Inverness-shire border; how soon, I wondered, would it be traversed by a road that would bring Speyside within easy reach of Deeside, a road that would fulfil the dream of General Wade more than two centuries ago, to link the barracks at Ruthven, near Kingussie, with Braemar?

The time was 10.15 a.m. We had been going now for more than three hours. And so far we had not even thought of putting on skis. I was not, however, to be allowed to escape for much longer. At the saddle beyond Carn Cloich-mhuillin— after a stepped descent that suggested to me the side of the Great Pyramid of Cheops—we reached snow at last, its surface hard, deep, unbroken.

I unfastened my skis from the sling round my neck, fitted them with skins and bent to clip them on. Then, very gingerly, I started to straighten up. Once I seemed to sway like a ship at sea and had to lean desperately on my sticks. I glanced at the others; they were chatting away gaily, completely unaware of this moment of anguish. Then at last I was vertical and could draw breath. It would have been inauspicious to fall flat on my back before we had even started.

From the col it was a continuous snow-slope all the way to the top of Beinn Bhrotain; a delightful climb, sun-warmed and exhilarating. Much of the crust was heavily iced and at one point early on our skis cut tram-lines across the surface of a frozen lochan. Beyond this the angle steepened sharply and we took a long diagonal, so long that I reckoned these must certainly be the eternal snows. It was difficult not to envy Theo's easy-looking style, long stride and powerful forward thrust combined in a perfection of rhythm obviously acquired under Norwegian masters. Every time a ski went forward, whether on the level or moving uphill, he would gain a few inches; not much, but always inexorably, something. The result was that very soon he—and John with him—were far in the lead. Toiling along in their wake, I felt unpleasantly like the losing crew in the Boat Race. The only consolation was that for most of the way I had Robert's company. He had no skins for his skis and in consequence had to endure the penance of a long and wearisome carry. As he and I reached the fringe of rocks at the summit plateau, a covey of ptarmigan took off, a sudden whirr of grey and white wings. Then, thankfully, we were at the twin cairns, the second a well-built wall rather than a cairn, enclosing the concrete Ordnance Survey block and providing a comfortable-looking resting-place for Theo and John.

Beinn Bhrotain (3,795 feet) is the eighth highest summit of the Cairngorms; west of the Lairig only the 'four-thousanders' Braeriach and Cairn Toul surpass it. It was also by almost 150 feet the highest point of our own day and we felt duly conscious of work well done. Of all the Cairngorms it is said to give the finest view down the Dee valley, but I cannot honestly say I noticed it; instead I was hypnotised by our first glimpse of the real test ahead—Monadh Mor and the immense white desert of An Moine Mhor, 'the great moss'. The farther rim of the latter, for which we were aiming, looked quite close, but I decided that the distance must be deceptive. Just how deceptive it was, we were to find out soon enough.

Coward-wise, I decided to keep the skins on my skis for the descent to the Monadh Mor bealach. The drop was almost 600 feet and I knew it would not be gentle; anything in the way of brakes to check an uncontrolled rush was much to be

Looking down Glen Geusachan to the Lairig Ghru.
The Devil's Point in the centre

desired. It was easy enough to fiddle about with my bindings to make quite sure I would be last away, at the same time sneaking a sidelong glance at the other three. Theo's judgment was masterly. He swung wide to the left, well clear of the scattering of rocks that stood out like fangs eager to snap at the first miscalculation. In beautifully controlled swings and christies he traced a route down the best of the snow until it was possible to work back on a long, straight traverse. Soon all three of them were out of sight on a bulge of steeper slopes below. My own take-off could be shirked no longer.

Fortunately it was unobserved, unless perhaps by a stray ptarmigan or two. Once under way I found the snow continuously tricky, in some places viciously iced, in others fluted and furrowed by the wind. The skins on my skis certainly checked my pace, but they made turning even more difficult than usual and I felt as ungainly as a crab on seaweed; no doubt I looked like one too. Leg muscles, strained unnaturally at each clumsy change of direction, were soon burning and aching in protest. It was only too obvious that for me the day's downhill running was to mean no respite and remarkably little pleasure. In spite of the added difficulty it was a relief to reach the steeper 100 feet curving finally into the white parabola of the col.

"Well done, old stager," laughed Theo generously as I fetched up at his side in one last melodramatic lurch. "You've made it all right so far."

"Not quite so much of the old stager," I managed to retaliate, forcing a sickly grin and bending shakily to remove my skis. "But thanks all the same."

The little saddle we had reached was our point of no return. Had the weather been bad, we should have been faced here with the choice between advance and retreat—quite conceivably a decision of some difficulty. As it was, the sun was shining free, there was no wind and the time was just after midday. The thought of going back never even entered our heads.

It was a delightful lunch-spot. Facing the sun, we looked out across a dazzling white corrie, a spacious amphitheatre where snow-blocks had broken from the eaves of the cornices above and lay scattered in confusion on the floor. In the opposite direction behind us an immense snow-bed, hardened to

Cairngorms crossing.
Resting on the Beinn Bhrotain – Monadh Mor col

concrete by the action of wind and frost, thrust outwards over
the scoop of another, steeper corrie, Coire Cath nam Fionn.
Here we looked over the edge into Glen Geusachan, 'the glen of
the firs', and across to the Devil's Point, a black frown of cliffs
creased and lined with snow. Higher, the background slopes
climbed to a drift of mist at 4,000 feet, just touching Cairn
Toul and the Angel's Peak—so called, it has been said, "to
keep the devil in his place".

After a quarter of an hour the younger members of the
party were obviously chafing to be up and doing again; the
glint in their eyes betrayed what they thought of prolonged
tea-breaks. So the old men had perforce to put a brave face on
things and make ready for a further spell of toil.

Whoever it was that gave Monadh Mor its name—'the big
hill of the gentle slope'—can hardly have been thinking of our
line of approach. The corrie on our right dropped almost
vertically from under a moulding of cornices and its edge
demanded considerable respect. The ascent which we actually
faced was sharp enough too—300 feet of snow so wind-hardened
that it might have been beaten with hammers. The angle was
never too high for our skins to grip, but it was touch and go in
places and the occasional slips we did make, upsetting our
rhythm annoyingly, showed the difficulty even a degree or two
more would have caused.

All the way up the sun lay hot on our backs. Ski-tips thrust
forward over a snow-crust that flashed like scattered diamonds.
Despite thumping hearts and protesting lungs we exulted to the
full in our wonderful luck with the weather.

Then quite suddenly it all changed.

The depression which, according to the forecasts, was liable
to be coming in over the Eastern Cairngorms, was obviously
on the march. Beyond the dip of the Lairig Ghru the clouds
had massed and thickened, and now there was no longer the
consolation of any pools of blue. Friendliness went from the sky
overhead. Glen Geusachan had taken on the black and white
streakiness of a badly exposed print and it was not long before
the only colour left was in the views far out to the south-west.
Already the snow at our ski-tips had become grey and lack-
lustre.

Up on the plateau of Monadh Mor we faced a further three-quarters of a mile to the summit. But now the rise was so slight as to be barely noticeable and we pushed forward more easily, moving in silence save for the hiss of our skis. Each of us seemed withdrawn in his own thoughts. Very steadily we made ground and the few feet of height. Then, at length, centred in a sprinkling of black rocks, the diminutive, snow-plastered cairn was at our feet. The time was 1.20 p.m.

We stopped and someone produced a bar of chocolate. Then we bent to remove the skins from our skis, muttering as we fumbled with iced buckles and thongs.

"Well, there you are," remarked Theo cheerfully, straightening up and waving a ski-stick towards yet another white desert that stretched out as far as ever before us. "There's the rest of the day's work for you. It looks a bit different from the last time I was here; but then that was in June."

An Moine Mhor, 'the great moss', is one of the most interesting features of the Cairngorms. A vast upland saucer, several square miles in extent and keeping for the most part above the 3,000-foot contour, it typifies the immense scale and the loneliness, and at the same time the incomparable freedom of the whole range. It is no mere desolation of peat-hags, a weariness of the flesh on a sun-baked summer's day; rather is it a place of pleasant going—fine sandy granite and springy turf, cushioned profusely with the vegetation of high-altitude alpines. The burns that have their birth on its sides flow to three great rivers, the Spey, the Feshie and the Dee, and among its knolls and hollows huge herds of deer roam. Those who have not experienced the atmosphere of An Moine Mhor have not yet learnt to know the Cairngorms to the full.

Under deep snow, as we saw it, the Great Moss seemed doubly impressive. North-westwards the rim of black crags overhanging the hollow of Loch Einich and, nearer at hand, the Christmas-cake cornices above the headwaters of the River Eidart made striking landmarks. Otherwise, however, the saucer had no distinctive features: at our feet it fell away gently into a vague grey void; immeasurably far away it rose as vaguely and as gently to the ridge of Carn Ban Mor, barely distinguishable from the leaden threat of the sky. This ridge we had to reach.

The start I made could not have been described as impressive. I had dispensed with my skins, but even so the initial descent should have been simple, for the angle was favourable and the run almost entirely one straight traverse. Everything, however, seemed to have combined in a sinister conspiracy against me—the patchiness of the snow, the deceptive lighting, my growing tiredness, even one of my skis which came adrift every time I fell. Soon the others were far ahead, slowing eventually to a halt on more level ground and waiting patiently while I stumbled behind in solitary exasperation.

Yet, strangely, it was just beyond this point that I had the most enjoyable running of the whole expedition. The light had become so bad—almost the equivalent of a complete white-out —that it was impossible to judge angles or measure humps and hollows. Somehow, all the same, I managed to stay upright for what seemed a remarkably long time, keeping well up with the others and even enjoying a few turns. This was mountain travel *par excellence*, to be spun out to the last pleasant yard.

"That was grand," I said breathlessly, as we slowed to another halt and took fresh stock of our position. "That's the kind of running I like."

"Well," replied Theo, "it was certainly a nice gentlemanly slope." From which kindly remark I gathered that it had been only just off the level.

I had expected that the crossing of the Great Moss would mean quite simply going down one side of the saucer and up the other. But it was nothing like as straightforward as that. The middle portion is both extensive and undulating, and we even found that some of the slopes were long enough to make it worth our while putting on or removing skins. We passed the trench of the Allt Luineag, the burn which rises at over 3,500 feet on Cairn Toul and makes the main source of the Eidart. It was bridged solidly with snow. Similarly all traces of Loch nan Cnapan, the little 'lochan of the knolls', seemed to be completely hidden. In our empty grey solitude it was impossible to picture the moor hereabouts under a blue summer sky, warm and coloured, the haunt of ptarmigan and golden plover. The only living things we saw were occasional flies or spiders on the snow, blown by the wind perhaps to the middle of this vast, inhospitable desert.

It is easier now, looking back on the expedition, to appreciate how fortunate I was to have such safe companions. Any kind of mishap in the middle sections of the crossing would have been thoroughly unpleasant; indeed anything at all serious in worsening weather might have involved us in quite a struggle for survival and was simply not to be thought of. But with Theo as leader the margin of risk had been reduced to a minimum. His own ski-ing was faultless and he had impressed on John and Robert that any sort of dash and crash technique could have no place in cross-country work of this kind; to this the youngsters had responded admirably. His biggest concern must have been my blundering, but if it was, at least he said nothing about it. Now it was in large measure thanks to him that, as we faced the last ascent of the day, we were still in excellent order.

The climb to the Carn Ban ridge must have been all of 2 miles. The slope was never steep, it just went on upwards; inexorably, dispassionately upwards, as though it had had no beginning and, as surely, would have no end. There was nothing near at hand by which to measure our progress; no peat-hags, no burns, no clumps of heather. The few protruding rocks, black pinpoints of skerries in a grey-white sea, might have been 10 yards away or 1,000 for all we could tell; they never came any nearer. The slow passing-by of four pygmies seemed to bear no relation whatever to the remote crags of Sgor Gaoith or the cirque of Braeriach's Coire Dhondail. It was not cold. There was practically no wind. But for much of the time fine snow fell, visible against the back of the man in front as it drifted lightly down. We could only guess what it would all have been like in driving mist or a blizzard. On and on we climbed, thrusting our skis mechanically forwards, endlessly up to the vague horizon of our ridge-crest.

And in the end there was nothing dramatic about our arrival. One moment we were plodding uphill, the next we had halted on a broad snowy shoulder, flat as a tennis-court. There was little comment, for we were past wasting words, only muttered approval when Theo produced his flask of tea and allowed us our second drink ration of the day—a quarter of a mugful each.

The slopes which hem in the east side of Glen Feshie have always had a special attraction for skiers. Long before the crowds came teeming to Cairn Gorm, or ski-tows and *pistes* were thought of, members of the Scottish Ski Club found scope for adventurous running on the plateaux and in the sweeping corries of Carn Ban and its neighbours. In particular the corries feeding the Allt Fhearnagan, 'the alder burn', which falls to the pine woods near Achlean, gained reputations as playgrounds, their huge snow-wreaths offering wonderful scope for fast homeward runs. We had all been looking forward to this final descent from Carn Ban as the highlight of the expedition, as recompense for the hard miles that had gone before. We were confident that it would round off the day with a memorable, exhilarating climax.

It was not easy to find the best starting-point. The whole stretch of west-facing slopes had become featureless under the sombre, lowering sky. The ridges had lost distinctness, the corries between all character. To left and right stretched the same peppering of black rocks on toneless grey snow. Fingers of mist kept straying downwards, as though anxious to reach the level of Glen Feshie itself.

We ski-ed down perhaps a couple of hundred feet to a promontory where underlying scree broke through the surface of the snow, then paused for further reconnaissance. Right at our feet stretched a magnificent unbroken ski-slope. Here was the obvious continuation. But it was set at a startlingly high angle, much higher certainly than I had expected. At mid-height it bulged out like a wind-swollen spinnaker, then slid off right-handed into a gully. The run-out below on a thin tongue of snow looked a very long way away.

For some minutes I indulged in the pleasure of picturing myself taking that slope as an expert would have done: nonchalantly pushing off; accelerating smoothly and swiftly into the fierce, breathless swoop over the bulge; here and there a check and split-second turn; momentarily out of sight under the snow-wall, then suddenly reappearing in a swaying crouch, flat out on the last narrow thread of the gully.

Then I picked up my skis and started walking down the ridge.

Some way down I stopped to watch the other three. Even at a distance it was obvious that they were enjoying themselves immensely. For the steeper sections they kept close formation, zigzagging methodically and making each turn with studied care. But once the angles had eased, the discipline that had served so well throughout the day went to the winds and they scattered to choose their own individual lines down the final few hundred feet. I was happy to be a spectator this time, no longer a drag on the party. It all looked so simple and yet such tremendous fun. Certainly this last downhill running was everything that might have been desired. We had been right in our anticipation; there could have been no more satisfying climax to the journey.

We joined up again on the heather, not far now from Achlean. Outside the farmhouse the two cars were parked; apparently everything had gone well with Thelma and Adam in their long drive round over Drumochter. They had spotted us high on Carn Ban and now they welcomed us to the luxury of deep armchairs and a blazing fire. Mrs. Clark, the farmer's wife, was losing no time in busying herself with one of the biggest teapots I have ever seen.

When eventually, in drowsy contentment, we continued on our way down the glen, the light was failing rapidly. Automatically we looked back towards the plateau of Carn Ban. Its edge was indistinguishable in the grey depths of the clouds. There was still little or no wind, but the mist-fringe was trailing lower across the vague face of the snow. Soon it would be quite dark.

Up there the solitude was complete.

INDEX